The Elephant in the Office

The Elephant in the Office

Super-Simple Strategies for Difficult Conversations at Work

Diane A. Ross

www.dianeaross.com
Published by Elephant Conversations Ltd.

Editorial services: Kathryn Calhoun, www.WickedCopy.ca
Illustrations: Nelson Dewey, www.NelsonDewey.com

ISBN 978-0-9918113-0-4

To Mom, for your love, your encouragement, and for showing me the way with your entrepreneurial spirit. You and Dad always believed in me and for this I am forever grateful.

Table of Contents

A Note From the Author

The use by you of this book (the "Book") is subject to certain understandings and the terms and conditions set forth below. By using the Book, you acknowledge that you have read and accept such understandings and such terms and conditions.

Diane A. Ross and Elephant Conversations Ltd. (the "Authors") have prepared the contents of the Book for informational purposes only, which is not intended to constitute advertising, invite an attorney-client relationship or serve as a source for legal advice. Since no legal advice is provided through the Book, you should not rely upon any information contained herein for any purpose without seeking legal advice from a duly licensed lawyer competent to practice law in your jurisdiction.

The Authors make no warranties or representations of any kind whatsoever concerning any information made available on or through the Book. The content of the Book is provided only as general information. The Authors disclaim all liability with respect to actions taken or not taken based upon such information or with respect to any errors or omissions in such information. More specifically, The Authors shall not be liable for any direct, indirect, consequential, special, exemplary or other damages of any kind whatsoever and howsoever caused.

The stories shared in this Book come from the Author's own life as well as the accounts of others that have been shared with the Authors. Certain stories are fictional and for illustrative purposes only. In order to protect confidentiality, most of the stories and accounts have modified and the names of those involved or affected have been changed.

Acknowledgments

I first want to thank Scottie Wright: Because of you this book has been written. You changed my life forever and started me on a journey of awareness and self-discovery. Your difficult conversations with me were a model for how things could be done and they have inspired me to be the very best "me" possible. You have given me the opportunity to find my passion and share it with others.

To Jacquie Howardson: You have been with me throughout this ride... name changes, concept changes, story changes and all the other changes! You wrote, re-wrote and re-wrote again and you made me laugh as you "spiced up" my stories.

To Kathryn Calhoun at www.wickedcopy.ca: Truly this book would never have been completed without your brilliant writing and editing. You brought a fresh perspective and you truly "get" what I'm trying to do. You showed me how to make my personality come through on the page so this could be a book that is inviting and approachable. You rock!

To my much-loved group of supportive and caring friends (you know who you are): I count on you to keep me going, make me laugh and keep me sane. I know I can always count on your support, your wisdom and the gift you give me of showing me my best self.

To my sister Cathy Manson: This project would never have been completed without you. You took care of mundane details, stayed up half the night writing and re-writing and kicked me in the butt when I was ready to quit. You were one of my earliest and most difficult conversations and I will be forever grateful that you were open and willing. You showed me that truly one conversation can totally transform a relationship. You can read my mind (which is no small feat) and I know you are one of my greatest cheerleaders.

My biggest thank you is for my family: To my sons Robert and James who have endured my many absences, my hiding out in the office and living through the drama involved in writing this book. To my husband Bill: you have given me your unconditional support to work on this project without expectations of my business. You allowed yourself to be a guinea pig as I learned what I needed to learn and you graciously allowed me to "feature" you in many of my stories. Your support as I chase my dream means the world to me. Thank you.

Introduction

"My friends, until you try, you don't know what you can't do."

- Henry James

Let's get one thing straight now: this book isn't about becoming a "communications expert." It is not about negotiating world peace or becoming an inspirational communicator the likes of Gandhi or Mandela (although that would be admirable and if you do, feel free to give me the credit!). It is not about being perfect, tactful or even nice.

This book is about learning the essentials of having success in those workplace conversations you dread: from having to tell someone their body odor is overpowering to talking to someone about their disrespectful behavior. It is about learning some fundamental tools that will allow you to manage tough conversations when you are in the "hot seat" and things are starting to go south. It is about giving you the confidence to handle whatever is thrown your way.

We have all had those conversations that ultimately give us such a resounding and unexpected slap in the face that they set our heads spinning... you know, those "I cannot *believe* you just said that to me!" or "What flippin' planet are you on anyway?"

conversations that ended so badly you either fled and licked your wounds or fought so hard your "angry vein" pulsated menacingly through your forehead. Let's not even mention those conversations where the only consolation was a jumbo-sized bottle of wine (any kind will do!). Now there is no end in sight for the cold war that has resulted.

Whenever you have one of those nightmare conversations, you may find yourself left saying, "I should have known better," or "Never will I go there again." Well, I am here to tell you that it is actually pretty darn important to "go there," because if you don't step up to the plate and tackle these conversations, things simply cannot ever get better. Unfortunately, you are dreaming if you secretly hope your stinky employee will get trapped in a perfume factory, your difficult boss will move to Australia or your snotty coworker will be hit by a bus. It is kind of like having a financial plan based on winning the lottery - nice to think about but overall kinda, well, stupid.

It has been my experience that the most difficult people in our lives never leave; we have to either deal with them eventually or continue on in stony silence and abject misery until we develop ulcers and less-than-sunny dispositions. If we don't have these tough conversations, inevitably productivity suffers, morale plummets, relationships sour and complaining becomes a regular pastime, further entrenching people in the ugly, unhappy problems they just don't know how to solve.

In my workshops, I frequently use lighthearted examples such as how to tell someone that they have B.O. or bad breath. More often than not, somebody pulls me aside at the end of the day and asks me if I had secretly been asked to cover that topic specifically because everyone knows that Joe or Cindy or whoever it might be that day has "that very problem." Everybody knows, of course, except the person in question. Now that would be humiliating! I think most of us would just want the "straight goods," even if it is embarrassing.

I wish I could say that there is a secret formula to prevent the other person from being upset, embarrassed or disappointed when we engage in these types of conversations; however, I have not discovered that magic formula yet (but if you do, call me because we need to talk book sequel!). What I *have* learned is that there are some simple tools we can use to get ready for these conversations. How we prepare, craft and deliver our messages and how we manage reactions can make these challenging conversations go a whole lot more smoothly. I have also learned that the more you practice using the communication tools I am going to share with you, the easier it becomes. These conversations may even start to feel natural.

What has been meaningful and even life changing for me and for many of those that I work with are the simplified tools I use for having successful conversations. This book is my spin on what I have learned and what has worked for me. When I started my journey, I found the material and research on difficult conversations daunting to say the least. I started to ask myself, "Am I ever going to be able to remember all of this stuff? Can I really do this? Is it possible I am the wrong personality type or that I require some kind of intensive psychotherapy if I want to communicate effectively?" Of course, you've already figured that these were just excuses. I did think about giving up, but I didn't because as I tested out some of the tools and strategies, I discovered they actually work. That progress gave me the motivation to keep plugging away at it.

In this book, I will share with you what I have learned. I have simplified the tools and highlighted some of the essentials so that you don't need to be a rocket scientist to have a tough conversation and be successful at it. Improving your communication skills *is* doable and, if you hang in there, you will see results. I don't want this to be like some fad diet that sounds great in theory but when you try to stick to it you feel like you're suddenly starring in *Mission Impossible* (sort of like the diet a girlfriend of mine attempted in high school: She was supposed to eat only grapefruit for six weeks. Not surprisingly, after a few days I'm pretty sure she was ready to pass out. She had to quit. But I digress...).

The prescription in this book is not a fad diet. Think of it as a lifestyle change in which you learn to have the confidence to say what you really want to say and actually get the results you want. It is about making small modifications and changes and seeing big differences over time.

Sound easy? It actually can be.

My Story

So, where did it all begin? How did a litigation lawyer like me become interested in real and respectful communication?

While at law school, I received distinctions for the oral presentation of my moots (mock trials) in both my second and third year. The partners in the established law firm where I started my career were clearly impressed. I knew I was destined for a successful litigation career when my first Supreme Court trial involved defending a dog that had allegedly bitten an elderly, sick woman. I am happy to report (I think) that I was able to convince the judge of the dog's innocence.

For 14 years I was on top, impressing colleagues, bosses and clients alike. I was a serious, accomplished multi-tasker. I practiced law, had a family and started and managed two successful businesses. No wonder friends and family say I do "chaos" well. Now, there were many things I loved about the practice of law, including the challenge of a rousing courtroom battle, but the mounds of paperwork and the tedium of preparation, not to mention the adversarial environment, were taking their toll on me. I began to question myself and my choices, what I could do, where I could go from here. It quickly became obvious: as a lawyer, was I not an expert in conflict resolution? Surely, I could take my legal skills into the field of difficult conversations and conflict management. It seemed to make perfect sense.

I began to devour armloads of information. I knew I was on the right path! I was right about what I was doing, right about what I was learning, right about everything in fact... or so I thought. The skills I had learned that were so critical to my success in the courtroom, i.e. constantly persuading others that I was always right, I soon realized do not work well in other aspects of life. I discovered that "being right" does not work at the negotiating table, is destructive to relationships at the office and is absolutely devastating to personal relationships. Fortunately for me, there was a faint glimmer of enlightenment at the end of this long, dark "I am always right" tunnel.

Right? Wrong.

A key moment for me in this "I may not always be right" journey was at a party I was invited to many years ago. It turned out that I did not know very many of the guests, but I had the privilege of sitting beside a very interesting and successful businessman. Unbeknownst to me, I was about to learn a very valuable - if humbling - lesson. He was asking me about the kind of work I did and (I admit it!) at that time I was pretty darn full of myself. I mean, I had accomplished a lot and most of it in a "man's world." I was regaling him with tales of a presentation I had just done entitled "I Am Right, You Are Wrong, or Is There Another Perspective?" It was a session about being accountable in workplace conversations. Of course, I did not think it applied to me, at least not at that stage. In retrospect, I must have been unbearable, although he never let on. He was fascinated, or at least I believed he was. He told me about his former partner, a woman who also happened to be a rather successful lawyer. They had been together for several years and, according to her, he had never been right, not once, during all the times they had disagreed. He pointed out to me that, statistically speaking, it is impossible for one person to be right 100% of the time. (Hello, Diane – is a light bulb going on yet?)

I realized in that moment that this was the approach that I had been taking when I got into any kind of disagreement. I assumed that I was right. My beliefs were right, my assumptions were right, my judgments were right. I was just plain right. The problem when I took this approach was that the other person went on the defensive and the conversation inevitably went sideways. This man's observation about the improbability of always being right caused me to begin to question myself - just a little. Was my apparent obsession with being right a contributing factor to the constant conflict I was experiencing in my relationships? Now *that* was food for thought. I learned that maybe, just maybe, turning every disagreement into a courtroom battle was not the answer.

What Is an "I" Statement Anyway?

Another critical "Ah HA!" moment on my journey happened when I attended the Executive Coaching Program at Royal Roads University. I thought it would be an interesting way to "unstick" myself and figure out exactly what is was I wanted to do in the field of conflict resolution. During the first few days of the program, I actually had the arrogance to think that they didn't really have much to teach me. I thought I was more educated, more sophisticated and obviously more skilled than my classmates. I was actually quite shameless when I think back (if you could see my face right now, you would see me blushing). I was suffering from a serious lack of humility and insight. Little did I know, everything was all about to change…

On the third day of the program, one of the instructors suggested we use "I" statements in our conversations and when coaching others. I put my hand up and asked, "What is an 'I' statement?" Everyone in the room went silent and many eyes turned to give me incredulous looks. Some eyes were cast to the floor. I felt that day that most of my colleagues in that class would have burst out laughing if they would have had the nerve. I was a bit perplexed and, in that moment, I realized I actually had some serious work to do. For those of you who do not know what an "I" statement is (and don't worry, I won't laugh!), here is your first hint: it is the opposite of a "you" statement, which often carries with it either a direct or indirect laying of blame. When we use "I" statements responsibly, we take ownership for what we are saying, rather than blaming someone else.

These may sound like "I" statements but sadly, they don't qualify:

✗ I think you are a jerk.

✗ I think you are wrong.

✗ I think you are unreasonable.

A proper 'I" statement may sound more like this:

✓ I felt humiliated when...

✓ I am concerned about...

✓ I believe that when...

(Don't worry too much about these for now; we'll talk about "I" statements in more detail a little later.)

Then Along Came My Bull-Riding, Straight-Talking, Unsuspecting Hero

My most profound eye-opening moment on my journey was an encounter with a wise man named Scottie whom I met during my coaching program. He changed my life forever and is now both a great friend and coach. I have to tell you that Scottie was not my usual kind of hero. He has a Ph.D. in agriculture, was a bouncer in his former life and rode bulls for fun as a young man - definitely not my type at all. Really, how could this man have anything in common with a know-it-all like me? Oh, I forgot to mention that he was also an expert in EQ (Emotional Intelligence) which, at that time in my life, seemed to be not much more than a bunch of irritating psychobabble.

So what made Scottie so special? Well, you've probably figured out by now that those around me found my somewhat arrogant attitude and behavior rather intolerable. The funny thing, though, was that when Scottie talked to me, he said the things that others lacked the courage to say. He was able to give me feedback about my (let's be truthful here) bad behavior in a way that was honest and direct. At the time, I was using one of our social gatherings as an opportunity to get some laughs at somebody else's expense (ugh, I know, not good!). Scottie pulled me aside and told me he was uncomfortable with the comments I had made and wondered if others may have felt the same. He asked me if I realized how I was coming across when I behaved this way and if that was the kind of person I wanted to be. He told me that he thought I deserved to know how he perceived my comments and my behavior.

Ouch! Initially, I was taken aback. I mean, what did I even care what Scottie thought? Well, as a matter of fact, I cared an awful lot; I was embarrassed and upset with myself. Eventually, though, I thought about what he had said and I could feel myself becoming grateful. His words were really hard to hear and more than difficult to digest, yet I left the conversation feeling respected and cared for. How could he have been so brutally honest without coming across as "I'm right and you're wrong?" He left me wondering how on earth he got me to question my behavior and perspective without shoving his opinion down my throat (as I was admittedly prone to doing myself).

How Did He Do It?

I soon discovered that I was not the only one who felt this way about Scottie. By the end of the course, I believe that just about every person I knew in the class had asked him for coaching. What did Scottie teach us? First, he taught us that it was possible to have tough conversations in a way that is direct (my preferred style), honest (I had this down most of the time) and respectful (this I was lacking). He did not use "hot" or judgmental language. He did not make assumptions; he simply shared what he observed and he owned his experience. He did not in any way present his version as being the only way or the "right" way of viewing the situation.

So what was my problem? Why was I floundering in almost every difficult conversation? Was it because the underlying theme in my communications was that I absolutely had to be right? If I ask myself now what being right ever got me, I can honestly say that grief, heartache and unresolved conflicts were constant companions for the entire time I employed the "blame-and-complain" method of communication.

All of these experiences showed me that there was another path. I could choose to be different in how I came across and how I managed my toughest conversations. I wanted to do what Scottie did so naturally and stop with the "being right" thing. I knew it was going to be a challenge, but I was sure I was up for it. Like you, I had some very important relationships at stake.

Back to the Books

I hit the books again (hey, it's a lawyer thing) and went into hyper research mode. I attended countless courses and read every book I could get my hands on relating to the topic of "difficult conversations." I went to Harvard Law School's program on negotiation for lawyers to take courses in mediation and managing difficult conversations (an amazing experience that I highly recommend).[1]

Years later I am still learning and, yes, I still mess up. It hasn't been easy; in fact it has been a real struggle because I have been constantly battling my instinct to be right, to be in control and to win. However, what I do know is that if I can learn this stuff, anyone can. If you asked me, "Is it worth it?" I would reply with a resounding, "YES!" It has made a huge impact on some of the most important relationships in my life: with my hubby, my sister, my mother, my children, my closest friends and my work colleagues. It has allowed me to say "no" to those I never believed I could say "no" to. Most importantly, improving my

"If you learn from defeat, you haven't really lost."

- Zig Ziglar [2]

ability to have difficult conversations has saved me a ton of time and mental energy that I used to spend either (a) agonizing over whether to bring something up, (b) replaying and reliving worst-case scenarios or (c) cleaning up the aftermath of horrible conversations that failed because I'd sunk to name-calling, judging and/or being defensive.

Writing Your Own Success Story

I want to share with you the tools I have learned along the way simply because I am passionate about this subject and would like to fast-track others towards their goal of successfully tackling difficult conversations in the workplace. Over the years, I have realized that many of us do not know how to have successful conversations because we do not have the necessary navigational tools for when things inevitably become challenging. We end up struggling, bogged down with assumptions and misconceptions about those we are trying to speak with. Business partnerships dissolve, conflicts with the boss abound and working relationships deteriorate to the detriment of the company. What is going on here? If I have ever been truly "right" about anything, it is that we all need to learn some tools to have those tough conversations so that we can get what we want without the extra strife and stress.

Help is on the way! There is a way to resolve those lonely late night conversations we have (with ourselves) just before we drop off into a troubled sleep. It is my hope that by learning some of the tools, skills and strategies that follow, you will have the courage to engage in your most dreaded conversations and stop putting them off - because nothing can change until you do.

Remember the magic of story time as a child? I am going to use stories to help illustrate what I have learned in the hopes that it will engage and entertain you, as well as teach you. The stories are mine, inspired from real stories or derived from others with ample modifications and name changes to protect the "innocent" (you know who you are!). I want you to have fun as you explore this book.

Study and implementing the very tools that I am going to share with you has given me confidence and a purpose and passion in my work. I have, without a shadow of a doubt, improved relationships not just at work, but in all aspects of my life. What more could a reformed "always right" lawyer ask for? My hope for you is that, as your conversation skills increase, you will gain inspiration and confidence, as I have. I want you to look forward to a time in which you will be able to say what you need to say in the workplace and manage those conversations that are most important to you, with the goal of improving your work relationships, lowering your stress and getting what you want out of your career. It isn't far off now!

Let's get started.

Chapter 1:

We Really Do Need to Talk...

Success in our everyday conversations is not usually that difficult unless it is one of "those conversations" we dread or one that starts off well and then slides sideways - quickly! You know what I'm talking about: suddenly you have a difficult conversation on your hands and you are not quite sure why or how it happened.

"I am an old man and have known a great many troubles, but most of them never happened."

- Mark Twain

What one person finds hard to talk about or handle, another may not. Based on my experience, a sure sign you need to step up to a tough talk in the workplace is if you are suffering from any or all of the following symptoms:

- [ ] Losing sleep at night
- [ ] Stressing about it during the day
- [ ] Complaining (be honest!) to anyone who will listen about the person and/or problem

These are conversations that, when you only think about them, you agonize and make yourself sick because you *know* you need to say something to somebody but you just don't know how to say it. Maybe it's a looming conversation with your boss, your client, your meddling coworker, your secretary... The list is endless, seriously.

Because this book focuses on workplace conversations, let's look at the kinds of conversations we struggle with on the job (although, as an aside, don't be surprised if you find that the techniques in this book apply to conversations outside the workplace, as well). We are going to cover the following types of conversations in detail throughout the book:

Delivering Sensitive News: Smelly Shelly

Imagine you are tasked with the job of telling Shelly that she has very bad B.O. Now, you like this woman and are wondering firstly why it has to be *you* who breaks the bad news and secondly how she could be so completely unaware of the awful "vapor trail" she leaves behind her wherever she goes. No one has done anything yet, so now the air is so thick with various air fresheners that the evening janitorial staff is wearing masks and the new I.T. guy's allergies are completely out of control.

You are the office manager and you really have no choice: it is your job to tell her. You have put the conversation off for days praying that somehow the problem will resolve itself. You and your boss have even had in-depth conversations about it behind closed doors. How could it be that she has such terrible B.O.? She seems to be very clean; could it possibly be her soap (you'd overheard someone saying she uses one of those "natural, organic alternatives")? Does she eat too much spicy food? What if you just left a small, anonymous gift of breath freshener and deodorant on her desk?

Sound familiar? How many of these kinds of discussions have we all had? I certainly have had more than I care to remember. The point is that none of these discussions are actually helpful; they waste our precious time and energy without solving anything. All of your guesses about why Shelly smells have gotten you nowhere and now you really do have to do something because your boss' minty-fresh breath is breathing down your neck. He does not want to work with Shelly any longer and clients are curling up their noses when she enters the room.

What could you possibly say to Shelly?

> "Shelly, I need to talk to you about something that is awkward. Lately, I have noticed you have had strong body odor. I am not sure if you are aware of it but I know if it were me I would want somebody to tell me." Now, STOP TALKING. (Resist the urge to babble; it will only make things more uncomfortable.)

Delivering Bad or Sad News: Fab Guy

Everyone loves Fab Guy. He is so funny and nice and is always ready to help out. In fact, he was always there whenever *you* needed him, which is why you had happily promoted him from graphic designer to manager of the division. Unfortunately, Fab Guy somehow just isn't getting the job done, despite the fact that his employees adore him and he is willing and cooperative. He has been giving his staff long extensions and flexible deadlines (hmm, no wonder they like him so much), which are affecting client satisfaction as well as the bottom line. You are dealing with the brunt of the fallout with clients and the rest of the executive team, and it is starting to wear you down. Fab Guy - bless his heart - acknowledges his role and his need to be "tougher" with his staff. You have worked tirelessly with Fab Guy to coach him about his management style, but not much has changed.

Fab Guy is optimistic things will improve shortly and tells you that he just needs a bit more time (but didn't he say that three months ago?). You are not so convinced that time is what is needed. What is keeping you up at night is your belief that Fab Guy is going to be devastated by the news; I mean, he's just so *nice*. But if you think he is going to be upset now, fast forward one year and imagine how this unfortunate conversation will go down then because that, my friend, is where you are headed. It is time to forget the past when you told yourself that you could turn Fab Guy into something he is not (ugh, you should have listened to your boss). You need to tell him now - not tomorrow or next week - that he is not the right fit for the management position; putting it off is not going to make it any easier. In fact, it will only serve to give you ulcers longer and make him more convinced he has what it takes, which will inevitably make the conversation harder. There is no way to tie this news up with a pretty bow; it's time to face the music and get this conversation over with.

What could you possibly say to Fab Guy?

> "Fab Guy, we need to talk. I don't think you are the right fit for the role of manager. The way I see it you have had trouble making tough decisions and holding staff to deadlines. Client projects have been delayed and those delays have had an impact on our reputation, not to mention the fallout with the executive team. You are a fabulous designer and incredibly well liked by everyone in this organization, which has made this an even tougher decision: I can no longer have you in the management role. However, everyone benefits from your creativity and if you are interested in going back to the position of graphic designer, it is yours. I know this is a difficult decision, so please take some time to think about it." Now, STOP TALKING. (Let your message sink in.)

Dealing With Rude or Disrespectful Behavior: The Big Cheese

You are the office manager in a small operation. Your boss, "The Big Cheese," has gained a (not unfounded) reputation for being pretty darn difficult to work for. He is arrogant, condescending and loves to blame others when things go wrong - and things go wrong all right! You are tired of his disrespectful behavior towards you and others. You are also fed up with being the human buffer/scapegoat/punching bag for him and the rest of the staff; all the griping and complaining from both sides is giving you migraines.

The Big Cheese's favorite and most upsetting trick is to embarrass you in front of your staff. He does this by disagreeing with you publicly, cutting you off mid-sentence or giving you his infamous exaggerated and exasperated glare. It has gone on for a long time, way too long, but you were finally galvanized into action after his most recent round of humiliating antics.

Here is how it went down: The discussion was about dealing with demanding clients. You started to share some of your insights and experience in dealing with this type of customer, but The Big Cheese fixed his steely glare on you and said, "This isn't about you, Denise. This is about doing the right thing for the client. Does anyone else have any thoughts or comments?" You were effectively silenced; tension descended over the room. The Big Cheese, completely oblivious to the atmosphere he had just created, said, "I think that Robert should take Mondays and devote a full hour to customer follow-up." You were (and are!) understandably upset; the Big Cheese didn't have an accurate picture of the problem and refused to listen to you - not to mention the fact that he has no idea how indispensable Robert is on Mondays!

You have finally decided that you need to say something, but how could you possibly talk to The Big Cheese?

"Big Cheese, I need to talk to you about how we interact with each other. Yesterday at our team meeting, I am not sure if you are aware, but when I was sharing my approach to dealing with demanding clients you said, "Denise, this isn't about you. This is about doing the right thing for the customer." You then went on to assign customer follow-up to Robert. I was humiliated because all of the employees were present. I believe that comment undermined my effectiveness as their manager. I am also wondering if you think I do not have anything valuable to contribute. What is your take on this?" STOP TALKING. (Let him respond.)

Dealing With Bad Behavior or Poor Performance: Marvelous Melissa

Your insanely competent, reliable and always dedicated office assistant has developed a strange new habit: she has been arriving late to your team meetings without having her financial reports completed. When she finally does get them done the work is, of course, stellar - you don't call her "Marvelous Melissa" for nothing! The problem is that decision-making is being delayed, meeting time is wasted and you have noticed that others are starting to make snide comments about Melissa's "special treatment" and referring to her as your "pet employee."

All of Melissa's excuses and your lack of action are making you look like an ineffective leader. You have tried to give a few hints to Melissa, to no avail. The last time you gingerly attempted to broach the subject, she explained that her dog had sadly eaten the report, which is why it wasn't done on time. You didn't know how to answer; didn't your kids try the same crap on you just last week? You silently wonder, Is Melissa taking advantage of our close relationship? Does she really think I am that gullible? You really can't afford to lose Melissa and sincerely don't want to offend the rest of your team. Quiet your inside voice and talk to her... but what could you possibly say?

> "Melissa, I am concerned. For the third time this month you have come to our team meeting late and without having your financial reports completed. The result is wasted time and the inability to move forward on upcoming projects. I am also concerned about the message it sends to the rest of the team. Your work is always excellent and this recent behavior seems out of character. I am wondering what is going on." STOP TALKING. (Find out her story.)

Saying "No:" Weekend Wanda

Your boss, Weekend Wanda, is completely disorganized, always scheduling last-minute crisis meetings and assigning huge projects late on Friday afternoons (due Monday at 8:00am!). You have obliged so far because you are ambitious and want to get ahead, particularly given the crummy job market. However, this weekend your 84-year-old granny is visiting from Kansas and you have already told Weekend Wanda that you will be unavailable for those 2 days. Since then, you have felt relieved that you had the courage to deal with this issue upfront before it became a problem... or so you thought.

Fast–forward to Friday at 4:30pm (you are due to leave at 5:00pm sharp to meet Granny's bus). Wanda comes into your office in a panic about a board presentation she has to deliver on Monday. She is desperate and you are apparently the only one who can help out. She needs you big time. You remind her that you are not available and, despite your earlier conversation, she appears absolutely shocked and disappointed. Then she starts in with the flattery and high praise for your work ethic, promising that the job will only take a few hours and you can squeeze it in while Granny is napping. You know better; after all, last-minute crises like this one are a dime a dozen with Weekend Wanda and always take hours (if not days) longer than expected.

Inside you are wavering, but you manage to say, "I'm sorry. I have had these plans for months." Well, *now* Weekend Wanda's eyes narrow and she resorts to subtle-but-scary threats, leaving you with the distinct impression that you can kiss your long-awaited promotion good-bye. Frustrated and emotional, you imagine your dear old granny spending the weekend alone watching soaps and trying to wrangle your badly-behaved golden retriever. You are caught between a rock and a hard place, here. Who could help but agonize over how to handle such an awful, unfair situation?

Take a deep breath and stand your ground because if you don't, you will set a dangerous precedent for the future. You could respond by saying:

> "Wanda, it sounds like this presentation is very important to you and you really want me to help out. Usually, I am keen to step up to the plate, but in this case I am unable to do that. My granny is visiting from Kansas and it is important to me that I spend this time with her." STOP TALKING. (Silence is definitely your power tool here!)

What Do These Conversations Have in Common?

Some conversations are obviously harder to deal with than others, especially when you're faced with communication that falls under more than one "type." However, the commonality between all of the conversations above is that there is something very big and important at stake. The question I ask myself when thinking about whether I need to engage in a tough conversation is: "What is at stake, here?" Is the issue at hand something that is important enough to warrant my speaking up?

Here are some examples of what topics might require a high-stakes conversation in your workplace:

"You are what you do when it counts."

- John William Steakley, Jr.[3]

Your leadership: If you are a supervisor or manager who does not deal with performance or behavioral issues with members of your team, it speaks volumes about your leadership skills and your ability to handle sensitive and/or difficult situations. People are looking to you to make those difficult decisions and take action; you owe it to them to act.

Productivity: More often than not, if we don't have these tough conversations, productivity suffers - especially when we are dealing with issues of performance or competence. Work doesn't get done (or doesn't get done properly and needs to be redone). In addition, employees spend an inordinate amount of time complaining, not only about the person who is causing the problem, but also about the supervisor who is not handling the situation (a.k.a. you or me!).

Your Self-Respect or Self-Esteem: If we do not speak up, we end up feeling disrespected or marginalized. It is simply a matter of principle. We need to stand up for ourselves when we feel that people have treated us in a way that is disrespectful or unkind. If you don't let people know how their behavior is negatively affecting you, how can things possibly change? Remember that awareness is critical; none of us can change what we don't know.

The Relationship: Is the relationship at stake? Think about it. If you do not deal with an issue that has come up between you and somebody else, here is what generally happens: resentment starts to build, assumptions get made and, pretty soon, we begin harboring some seriously negative feelings toward the person in question (and vice-versa). Imagine how the relationship will suffer if you never talk to your colleague about her constant texting when you go out to lunch together. You start to make judgments: She is rude. Her behavior is inappropriate. She is immature and inconsiderate of you and your time. She must not really value your relationship at all. Maybe you're right or maybe you're missing something, but either way does that sound like the makings of a healthy relationship to you? I didn't think so.

When ruminating over whether to bother having a difficult conversation, remember to ask yourself what is at stake. Is the quality of your leadership at stake? Is business productivity at stake? Is your self-respect or self-esteem on the line? Is there a relationship that will suffer? If the answer is "yes" to one or more of those questions, you probably need to step up and have that conversation. Once it's over, chances are good that you will sleep better and worry less, too!

Top Tools to Recall: Determining When You Need to Talk

- ✔ Step up to a tough conversation when there is something important at stake.
- ✔ Knowing that there is something important at stake can give you the courage to have the conversation.

Great! Now you are sure there is something important at stake that requires a serious conversation (but maybe you suspected as much already). You want a positive outcome - but how?

We will get to that, I promise... but first, let's look at the single worst thing that almost *all* of us do that gets in the way of our success. Until we understand the role this nefarious little habit plays in messing up our work relationships, career and emotional well-being, we may not truly have the inspiration and courage we need to step up and talk.

Curious? (Ha, my evil plan is working!) On to chapter two!

Chapter 2:

Avoid at Your Peril

Does Samuel Johnson's quote strike a chord with you? You've put off that dreaded talk (you know the one!) for so long now that you are feeling irritable and maybe even a little nauseous. You dread the thought of running into the offending person at the photocopier or your local lunchtime sushi hangout. Hey, if you can just avoid the person for a few more years, then maybe the issue will go away on its own!

"Courage is the greatest of all virtues because if you haven't courage, you may not have an opportunity to use any of the others."

- Samuel Johnson

Avoidance isn't the answer, as much as you might hope it will be. We would like to think that if we buried our heads in the sand, our woes would evaporate. Well, my friends, it didn't work out for the ostrich and it definitely didn't work out for this poor guy:

Brazilian Loses More than Hearing

A 39-year-old Brazilian man went to a medical clinic complaining of muffled hearing. While in the waiting room he believed he heard his name called, so off he went into the examination room with the doctor. The doctor and the staff prepared and treated the patient, but in an area nowhere near his ear; the man left the clinic with a vasectomy and no resolution of his muffled hearing! How did it happen? Apparently, he did not ask any questions during the procedure. He later told staff he thought that perhaps his ear inflammation had reached as far as his testicles![4]

If only this poor gentleman had read chapter one of this book, he would have known this was one conversation with very high stakes! All kidding aside, this is a mind-boggling example of how keeping quiet at critical times does not do anyone any good. Even a simple observation or comment on his part ("Are you sure this will help my hearing?" or "Oh, I didn't know you could fit hearing aids down there!") would have halted the procedure and saved him his fertility. Obviously, this man did not feel comfortable questioning the authority of a physician - and the consequences of avoidance here were unfortunate to say the least.

FYI: If you are still fantasizing that your arrogant boss will relocate to far-flung lands or that your snotty coworker will be done in, you are not only deluding yourself but you are practicing closet avoidance - big time. Most of us could write a book on the conversations we've avoided and the subsequent disastrous results. Perhaps our stories of avoidance are not as dramatic as the story of the Brazilian man above, but that doesn't mean that avoiding an important workplace conversation can't send the wrong message or have undesirable consequences.

Here's an example of what I'm talking about: I call it "Gorgeous Gal and Dan the Man."

You are a young and ambitious female business grad. Each year, High Tech Inc. hires about 20 interns and you made the cut (congratulations!). You are ecstatic and feel a strong need to prove yourself both in terms of your work and whether you are a good fit for the team because only five people are going to be offered jobs at the end of the internship.

One day, you get your big break: you have a chance to work with one of the hotshot project leads: Dan the Man. It is going to mean weekends and late nights, but it is an exciting project and an amazing opportunity. You start working with Dan the Man and things seem to be going well. He is charming and smart and very complimentary of your work. He also often remarks on how nice you look and, although you feel flattered, you don't think too much of it. Then, one day, he tells you he thinks you have great legs. You can't help but feel he has crossed the line and are a bit uncomfortable about the comment. You don't quite know how to respond, however, so you say nothing.

"My dear friend, clear your mind of can't."

- Samuel Johnson

A few days later you are out at a client dinner with Dan the Man and a few others. Dan is right next to you and all of a sudden - OMG! - you feel his leg sneakily touch up against yours. You think to yourself that it must have been accidental, but then it happens again. You are extremely uncomfortable and quickly move your leg away, but his leg follows yours like that icky enamored skunk from *Looney Tunes*; you feel completely trapped. After all, you are at a client dinner; short of grinding your Jimmy Choo stiletto into his tootsies (which would cause a nasty scene) or flee the restaurant (which would come off as beyond unprofessional), what could you do? Feeling helpless, you don't do or say anything - again.

Sadly, this is an all-too-common story. You've just done what any self-respecting low-on-the-hierarchy ambitious women would do (I know I certainly have): absolutely nothing. You try to convince yourself that it is not a big deal, but deep down you know that boundaries have been crossed - and there is a lot at stake here. Yes, it is true that if you talk to Dan the Man you may risk your "ideal job." On the other hand, your self-esteem and self-respect are on the line. If you avoid saying "no" when you need to, no matter how you think the conversation will go, it sends the message that you are okay with the other person's behavior and there is a very real possibility things will get much worse.

So what could you possibly say to Dan? Here are some options:

> "I need to talk to you about what happened at the client dinner the other night. I am not sure what your intentions were but when you touched my leg under the table I was uncomfortable." STOP TALKING. (Less is more.)

Or you could say:

> "Dan, I wanted to clear the air about something that has been bothering me. When you made the comment about my legs the other day and then touched my leg at the client dinner last night I felt uncomfortable. It is really important to me that we keep our relationship professional." STOP TALKING. (Hear him out, if he has anything to say.)

Or, if you are feeling very confident in the moment you might turn to Dan in a quiet voice and say:

> "Dan, I am a little uncomfortable with you touching my leg." STOP TALKING. (Silence shows confidence.)

Complaining: the Surest Sign You Are Avoiding

Complaining is a clue that you are avoiding a talk you really need to have. You can complain to your best friend or hound total strangers in the coffee shop and, sure, it feels good to vent, but take my advice and don't turn it into a sport. The main problem with complaining is that we become entrenched in the very problem we want to resolve. We usually complain to those who are sympathetic to our point of view or those who will understand our sorry plight. They agree with us wholeheartedly and that reinforces our idea that we are "right." The more outside reinforcement we get, the easier it is to convince ourselves that the other person is being rude or disrespectful. We start to make all sorts of assumptions and judgments, which only serves to make us more upset and miserable. The problem with this situation is that nothing is resolved and we end up with more stress, more ulcers, more tossing and turning.

To illustrate, let's look at a work scenario most of us can relate to: the ubiquitous "Chatty Cathy."

You work in an open space environment and Chatty Cathy often comes into your workspace, chatting in a very loud voice with her peers. It's been going on for ages and you hate it; you can't concentrate on your work and find it tough to talk on the phone with Chatty Cathy's constant babble in the background. You have tried to give subtle hints that her chit-chat is bothering you. You have pointed sharply to the phone receiver when you are on it, hoping she will get the message and lower her voice. You have even tried covering your ears melodramatically so that she would simply *have* to notice... and yet somehow, she hasn't. Obviously, this woman is as thick as a brick; she certainly doesn't seem to be getting the hint(s).

You don't want to seem petty or difficult so you don't actually say anything, but every passing day brings you one step closer to blowing your top and causing a legendary office scene in which you enact one of the many ways you have plotted Chatty Cathy's demise. Instead, you and your other coworkers complain bitterly behind Chatty Cathy's back about how rude and inconsiderate she is. You are feeling more and more upset and resentful about the whole thing and, as a result, your own productivity is suffering. Your relationship with Chatty Cathy is ultimately at stake here (not to mention your sanity); and yes, maybe you don't want to be her BFF and braid each other's hair at sleepovers, but you *do* still have to interact with her every day at the office, so for the sake of your peace of mind at work, it's better if you two can figure out a way to coexist.

The problem, of course, is that Chatty Cathy probably has no idea that her chatter is bothering people because nobody has actually had the courage to speak up about it to her directly. Doesn't she deserve to know? She definitely does and, more importantly, she can't change what she doesn't know. It is highly unlikely you are going to have any resolution of this or any other problem unless you step up to the plate for your tough talk.

Complaining puts you deeper into the problem, without any hope of resolution. In fact, things will probably get worse. Of course, I don't expect you to quit complaining cold turkey - even *I* admit it's kind of fun. However, I do have a compromise that I worked out with my close friend Jennifer; we call it the "two-minute whine rule" and here's how it works: I ask if I can have two minutes to whine and complain bitterly about something. If she agrees (which she always does - she is a good friend after all!), then I rant and rave for two minutes. At the end of the two minutes, she asks me a question that helps me to be proactive, stop avoiding and hopefully step up and have a tough conversation with the person in question.

Helpful Hint: The Two-Minute Whine Rule

Whine and complain for two minutes and then choose one of the two questions below to answer:

1. So, what are you going to do about it? *or*
2. What are your next steps?

I have worked in many organizations of varying sizes in different cities and countries, and a consistent theme I have experienced in all of them was the prevalence of complaining. It results in wasted time, negative feelings and loss of creativity, not to mention it entrenches people in the very problems that they would actually prefer to solve. Complaining, although it may feel good temporarily, is deadly both for our work relationships and for our ability to get things done. If we all could just embrace the two-minute whine rule, we would be so much more productive and would ultimately feel more content at work. If you find yourself regularly complaining to anyone who will listen, stop and ask yourself if you are having your conversations with the right people. I suspect the answer is probably no!

The Big Deal About Avoiding

Some people would like to think that *not* talking about their problems is a sign a maturity... but if you stoically manage not to talk to the person you have an issue with, does that really mean you are the "bigger person?" I don't believe so. The problem when we avoid a difficult conversation is that there is a lack of resolution and worse, we send a message to the other person that we are "a-okay" with whatever is going on. We then think we can cleverly contain our irritation, frustration and resentment, but these negative emotions inevitably leak out in our tone, body language and often in little snide comments we make. We say not-so-funny, thinly-veiled things like: "What time do you anticipate the arrival of the report finishing fairy?" or "There must be a short-sighted office rat in the lunch room – my favorite cheese has disappeared *again*!" Comments like those don't get the message across, even though you feel like you're laying it on pretty thick. The other person may think you are just being neurotic or attempting a lame joke.

"If you have time to whine and complain about something, then you have the time to do something about it."

– Anthony J. D'Angelo, author of Rich Grad, Poor Grad[5]

When we avoid a tough conversation, we create an "elephant in the office" that no one wants to address. In the long run, you will inevitably damage the relationships you were trying to preserve by *not* talking. Irritation and resentment will build and you will either explode or implode, but either way it is not going to be pretty. It reminds me of the pressure cooker we had growing up.

One day the cooker was left on far too long and the pressure was so great that it exploded, sending spaghetti sauce everywhere - the ceilings, the walls, the kids... *everywhere*. What a mess!

Here is a story about my sister, Cathy (not to be confused with Chatty Cathy!), who put herself in the proverbial "spaghetti sauce explosion" situation by putting off a conversation for far too long.

The Showdown: My Sister vs. Know-It-All Ken

My sister and I were attending an intense multi-day communications workshop. One participant - let's call him "Know-It-All Ken" - had been providing his point of view along with his frequent opinions throughout the entire workshop. Frankly, he was quite annoying. He interrupted the workshop leader and fellow participants so often that everyone visibly cringed when he opened his mouth to speak.

Towards the end of the workshop, we were doing a group wrap-up and review exercise with all of the participants and, little did Ken know, he was about to meet his fate. Blissfully ignorant, he rambled on and on, describing his views, his solutions and how he would do things differently. Ken was completely oblivious to the fact that others may have had something to offer; he blathered on and interrupted people constantly, driving everyone crazy and my sister to her boiling point.

Now Cathy had been complaining bitterly to me and others throughout the workshop about this behavior (others were complaining too), but said nothing to Know-It-All Ken or to the workshop leader about her frustration. I could see her getting more and more irate and, knowing her as I do, I feared it was about to get ugly - *really* ugly.

After days of avoidance, Cathy made up her mind to speak on behalf of everyone (without their permission - oops!) and tell Ken about the impact of his loudmouth behavior on the group. Using lots of "hot," judgmental language, she said, "Ken, you are being incredibly rude. You interrupt the leader constantly when we all would like to hear what he has to say. You keep jumping in with your views and don't allow anyone else to speak. I would really appreciate it if you would stop interrupting all the time." Way to go, Cathy, you really told him like it is. Yikes!

Well, you could have heard a pin drop in the room. We were all squirming in our seats, wanting to be anywhere but at that communications workshop (gotta love the irony). It doesn't take a psychic to predict that Ken's back would be waaaay up; he immediately went on the offensive. I will spare you the verbal play-by-play, but suffice it to say that it wasn't pretty. The workshop ended awkwardly to say the least, with a big fat elephant in the room. Nothing was resolved and tensions ran high. Nobody could get out of there fast enough.

How Could She Have Dealt With It?

Cathy had had something worthwhile to say and probably only said what everyone else must have been thinking. However, her message did not get through to Know-It-All Ken because she went on the attack by calling him "rude" and using accusatory language. She handled it poorly and, as a result, undermined her message and her credibility, which made her look foolish and caused nothing but hostility from Know-It-All Ken.

Many years later, Cathy understands the part she played and the overarching lesson: avoid at your peril. At some point, the pressure will be too great and you will eventually explode, just like that pressure cooker full of hot, messy spaghetti sauce, which will splatter all over you and a room full of innocent bystanders. This situation would have been better handled as a private conversation with Know-It-All Ken, preferably much earlier in the workshop, or she could have asked the workshop leader to deal with the problem before her blood boiled over.

To avoid a situation like this in your own life, be sure to check yourself for the following symptoms of avoidance:

- ☐ Constant complaining to anyone who will listen
- ☐ A naïve belief or desperate hope that your problems will resolve themselves spontaneously
- ☐ Recreating worst-case scenarios and running them through your head on repeat
- ☐ A "things will never change" mentality
- ☐ A slow, menacing simmer inside of you (that can't be blamed on the spicy food you ate last night!)

Why So Many of Us Looooove to Avoid

This is a biggie! We avoid some conversations because they are uncomfortable and we are afraid of how the other person might react. We are afraid of creating negativity in our work relationships or work environment as a result of our speaking up. We worry about opening a can of worms and causing irreversible damage. We don't want to come across as difficult, unsupportive, petty or presumptuous - and we absolutely, positively dread the thought of a painfully long, drawn-out conversation.

"F.E.A.R.: False Events Appearing Real" - Zig Ziglar

"Afraid." "Worry." "Dread." Sound fearsome to you? That's because fear is at the root of nearly every workplace conversation we choose to avoid. To circumvent the issue of fear, I remind myself that my fears are never as real or as scary as I build them up to be in my head. More often than not, I am pleasantly surprised by how much easier these challenging conversations are than I had anticipated. I also frequently have clients tell me with a sigh of relief, "That was so much easier than I thought it would be. I wish I'd had that conversation a long time ago!"

Don't fret if this doesn't feel 100% organic at first. It might not happen right away, but the more you practice, the more confident you will become. You may even find that having these conversations becomes natural, as if facing your toughest talks head-on were second nature to you (Wouldn't that be so nice?). Avoid telling yourself that you can't do it; that's just your fear talking. If you continue to work through this book and practice what you learn, you *will* get there.

Top Tools to Recall: Avoid at Your Peril

- ✓ Silence when you need to speak up can have serious, unintended consequences.
- ✓ Avoiding the conversation tells the other person that you are a-okay with their behavior.
- ✓ Complaining is a strong clue that you are avoiding a conversation you need to have.
- ✓ If you avoid for long enough, the stress will build up and you may end up exploding like a pressure cooker!

We now know that when there is something important at stake, avoiding the conversation flat out doesn't work (and in fact often makes things worse).

"People are much more likely to act their way into a new way of thinking than think their way into a new way of acting."

- Richard Pascale[6]

From here on, we are going to focus on what *does* work. I am about to share with you my four super-easy steps for your tough talks. If you follow these steps as well as the wealth of other tools you will uncover in the chapters that follow, you should be able to finally answer that all-important question: "How can I say this with confidence and get the results that I want?"

It isn't rocket science; it just takes preparation and practice. I am here to help you with the preparation part at least - so onwards and upwards!

Tame the Elephant in the Office
(in 4 pretty easy steps)

Step 1: Prepare to Talk

Get clear about what the real issue is and write it down in three sentences or less. Then determine what your ultimate goal is for the conversation. Be realistic.

Step 2: Design and Deliver Your "ABC Message"

What do you say and how do you say it? It's as easy as "ABC:" make it Accurate, Brief and Clear. Don't waste your time dancing around the issue; be honest and give people the "straight goods" in a way that is respectful and nonjudgmental.

Step 3: Stop Talking and Start Listening

Once you have delivered your ABC message, listen without interruption to hear the other person out. This may be your toughest challenge, but it is essential to keep the conversation on track... and it is easier than you think!

Step 4: Respond Powerfully

This is your opportunity to respond (not react) and clarify in a way that is confident, concise and clear. No excuses. No justifications. No blame.

Step 1:

Prepare to Talk

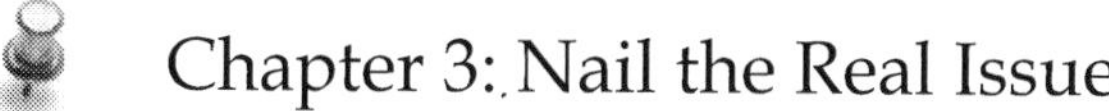

- Chapter 3: Nail the Real Issue
- Chapter 4: Hammer Out Your Goal
- Chapter 5: Resist the Temptation

Chapter 3:

Nail the Real Issue

Chapter highlights:

- ☐ *What is the person saying or doing (or not saying or doing) that is causing a problem for you?*
- ☐ *Separate fact from fiction – just the cold, hard facts!*
- ☐ *Be aware of how your assumptions, judgments and beliefs influence you.*
- ☐ *Implement the two-minute whine rule as needed.*

My "Sad Sewing" Story

When I was in ninth grade, my mom thought it would be a good idea if I took sewing. I was a bit skeptical as I was not the craftiest person by nature; she had already tried to teach me to knit once and that had been a disaster. Anyway, I got into a lot of trouble in sewing class because I always wanted to leap in and start, with no preparation. I would

> "Insanity: doing the same thing over and over again expecting different results."
>
> \- Albert Einstein

quickly hack up the fabric and then run to the sewing machine and line up the pieces using the "eyeball" method; then I would put the sewing pedal to the metal. At first, there would be great satisfaction... but then suddenly the sewing needle would careen off the garment and make a mess of the stitching. I would then have to go through the tedious task of ripping out all of the stitching and starting over. It was time consuming and exasperating. The sad thing is, most of my garments looked like old rags by the time I was finished and I would actually take *longer* than the students who took their time because of all the sewing I would have to redo. If only I had slowed down, prepared and planned ahead, I could have saved myself so much time and grief.

The same principles apply when tackling our challenging conversations. Don't approach your conversations the way I approached my sewing - you will not be happy with the result!

When we think about how to have a tough conversation, we often get overwhelmed and fail to make any progress. Now is the time to stop spinning your wheels and get grounded - and the first step is to nail down the real issue. Sometimes the issue is easy to define, such as having to tell somebody they did not get the promotion or needing to fire someone. Other times, defining the issue is trickier. If you are having trouble getting clear about the issue at hand, then ask yourself what the other person is saying, not saying, doing or not doing that is causing a problem for you or others. What precisely is it that is driving you crazy?

When relationships are strained, that strain complicates things and you can lose sight of what you are actually concerned about.

However, it is critical that you nail the issue down early because our emotions and our imaginations tend to run away with us, which can obviously make things much worse. We have a tendency to define issues in terms of what other people are "doing wrong" or some imagined character flaw of theirs. We make assumptions and are quick to judge.

Here is an example of a common way people define their issues when they have not yet nailed down the real problem: "Oh, the problem is my egomaniac boss is absolutely going to freak out when I tell him I'm not coming to his 'promotion party' because I'm away in Palm Springs. He thinks he's such a rock star, as if he is the most important person in the world. Seriously, does he really think we all can drop our plans just to accommodate his?"

"Labels are for filing. Labels are for clothing. Labels are not for people."

- Martina Navratilova[7]

News flash: describing your boss as an egomaniacal wannabe rock star is a judgment on your part, not an actual problem. To get a clearer picture of what's going on, you must ask yourself what your boss is doing or not doing that is causing a problem for you or others. Without asking the right question, you are assuming that if you do not attend your boss' party, it may negatively affect your relationship with him and your chances of getting that promotion. You actually need to *talk* to your boss about your plans and concerns - instead of preemptively inventing an issue.

Here is another example of how people commonly describe a so-called issue in the workplace: "If I leave this report for Lazy Linda to do, it will never get done. If I want to get anything done around this office I have to do it myself; I just don't have a choice." Oops - you have just defined the issue as Linda being "lazy" and taken on the martyr role by running in to save the day. Unfortunately, these are just your judgments, assumptions and beliefs once more, not an accurate assessment of the real problem. Again, ask yourself what Linda is doing or not doing that has led you to the conclusion that she is lazy - and how is Linda's action (or non-action) causing a problem for you or others?

Defining a problem as a shortcoming in the other person is a surefire way to put that person on the defensive, which creates instant trouble for the conversation. We often default to the "avoid/complain" option because it is the path of least resistance. Imagine how your poor friends feel listening to you go on and on about your self-important boss or sloth-like coworker. Ugh! I am sure they have heard quite enough. Remember the two-minute whine rule we covered in chapter two? First, you take two self-indulgent minutes to whine and complain to your trusty "whine buddy." Then it is time to move on and get proactive.

Identifying the real problem or issue essentially comes down to two questions:

1. What is the person doing or not doing that has led you to your conclusion or judgment? For example, if you say that Linda is lazy, then ask yourself what it is specifically that Linda does or doesn't do that leads you to the conclusion that she is lazy. (Stick to the facts please!)

2. How is the person's behavior causing a problem for you or others? For example, specifically *how* is Linda's behavior creating an issue for you or your coworkers?

Uncovering the Cold, Hard Facts

To answer these questions, we need to be real about what is going on and set aside our own colorful stories. The first part of identifying the issue is separating out the facts from our "Hollywood version" of what has been going on.

> "...begin challenging your assumptions. Your assumptions are your windows on the world. Scrub them off every once in a while or the light won't come in."
>
> - Alan Alda[8]

So what *are* the cold, hard facts? Stating the facts can be very tricky because inside us all are truly excellent story-making machines. Unfortunately, our stories are often full of assumptions and contain all sorts of "hot," judgmental language. Our extremely talented - yet often misinformed - inside voices help us to create these stories. You know the voice I'm talking about; it's that annoying little voice that chatters endlessly in our heads, acting as our own personal spin doctor, never at a loss for words and always eager to state an opinion. It takes the facts, reinvents them and creates a very colorful, one-sided story. The resulting concoction serves only to fan the flames and, just like any story, the more you play it and replay it the more believable it becomes. Your inside voice plays the blame game, worships the martyr and embraces the role of the victim. If you start to believe that your stories are "the facts," then you get stuck and it becomes very difficult to communicate without blame and criticism spewing out in your words and/or body language. Dealing with the inside voice takes practice, but it *is* possible to silence it with a little persistence.

Imagine how the conversation with Lazy Linda would go if you told her outright that she is not doing her fair share of the work. It is not going to go well unless you let go of all of the annoying, judgmental ideas your inside voice has accumulated and filed away as "very important and true information." Look hard for the real facts in your story. Be as specific as possible and describe the issue in three sentences or fewer. I know, that's a tough one; we all think that the more we have to say, the better. Nothing could be further from the truth. I am serious here: three sentences to describe what it is that the other person is doing, maximum!

Problem or No Problem: Just Think Before You Speak!

Please don't even consider opening your mouth until you have really separated out "your story" from "the real story." This may also require that you have a mental dump of all of your assumptions, judgments and beliefs to silence your nattering inside voice. Consciously dumping it out may prevent it from inadvertently leaking out while you are having the conversation. I will tell myself, "Diane, dump all that chatter and flush it." You will feel so much lighter (even if the scales do not agree!), clearer and better able to tackle the issue at hand.

I remind myself of the importance of the mental dump thanks to my own painful personal experience. We have all been there, blurting something out and, as the words fly across the room, wishing there were some way to rein them back in. It doesn't help that others are usually there to witness your disgrace - so, I am here to strongly encourage you to learn your (and my) lesson to take the mental dump before you speak.

Scary Secretary

Early in his medical career and just as early in my legal career, I received a frantic phone call from my hubby one morning. His new secretary had had a nervous breakdown and had abandoned ship. He was left with a full office, a busy day of patients and an empty reception desk. He sounded very nervous and stressed. After a bit of begging and some pitiful imploring, I checked my schedule and decided I could come in for the day and bail him out. (Aren't I the best wife ever?)

So, off I trotted to his office to save the day. As fate would have it, however, the job was much more difficult than I had anticipated, full of tedious details, frequent interruptions, irritable patients, endless phone calls and questions that I was nowhere near qualified to answer. In short, it was chaotic and I was madly scrambling to get things rolling. With impeccable timing, hubby buzzed me at the front desk. It rang 10 times before I could pick it up; who stays on the line that long anyway? (This was my inside voice, which was definitely not helping right then!)

"Can you get Dr. Smart from the Eye Bank on the phone for me?" hubby asked. "I have a patient who needs a transplant." Despite the relatively innocuous request, at this point my inside voice was screaming, "Are you *kidding* me? Are your fingers broken? Who do you think you are, you arrogant twit? How dare you ask me to do such a menial task - especially when I am out here busting my butt and doing you a *big* favor?" Now, this is where I should have taken a deep breath and taken a big mental dump. Instead, I blurted out in a loud voice in front of the entire waiting room, "Are you serious? Phone him yourself!" and I slammed the phone down - hard. (Slamming down phones was far more satisfying in the days before cordless technology.)

I looked up and saw that all of the patients in the waiting room were staring at me in complete disbelief. That put into context for me what I had just done. First, let's figure out the real issue here, which is easy enough: I was upset when hubby had asked me to make the call because I was overwhelmed at the time and the request seemed like an unnecessary, menial task... but instead of blowing up, when he had asked me to make that call I could have quite simply said - after the mental dump - something like this:

> "I am sorry, but I really don't have the time to make the call right now. I am just coping with the front desk." STOP TALKING. (You have made your point; no need to blab on.)

Taking that mental dump before you even open your mouth means you won't blurt something that is rude and aggressive.

Let's look at some work situations to see how we might go about this first stage of preparing for our own tough talks.

Setting Expectations: New Manager on the Block

Imagine that you have recently been promoted and you are now supervising a number of individuals who were your coworkers just last month. Coffee, lunch and the bar on Friday night used to be your norm with these people - now that you are the boss, things have gotten a little awkward. On Monday, at your first-ever team meeting, you clearly set out some expectations and priorities for the week ahead. Specifically, you assigned a number of your staff to work on a particular project for the week and you left the meeting certain that everyone was on the same page.

Fast forward to Friday at noon: it has come to your attention that one team member, Al, has not been working on your assigned project. You are fuming and your inside voice starts to chatter like crazy: "Al is a difficult employee. He has always been a slacker and he just *loves* to test his supervisors. Just because I'm new, he thinks he can push me around..." and on and on, spewing out all sorts of judgments. Despite how you may feel about Al, your inside voice really is not doing you any favors at this moment.

Take a step back and work on separating fact from fiction by questioning your version of the story. Ask yourself, "What is Al doing or saying that is causing the problem?" and do your best to answer truthfully. The facts may sound something like this: Al was your coworker a month ago; now you are his boss. You assigned all members of your team to work on a particular project this week and Al did not follow through. You do not know why he didn't work on it although you have some assumptions. Stop right there - those are the facts in exactly three sentences. (Remember, you only get three sentences or less.)

Next, ask yourself, based on facts only, how Al's behavior is causing a problem for you or others. As a new manager, you may define the problem as a concern about how accountability and communication are viewed by your team. If team members choose to work on other projects without informing you (for whatever reason, even if it is legitimate) what does that say about your leadership to both Al and the rest of the team? You are concerned that unless you deal with Al's insubordination, you are setting an unwelcome precedent for the future. Essentially your leadership, your self-respect and your relationship with Al and the rest of your team are at stake.

Now that you have a clear picture of the problem, what could you say to Al?

> "Al, I want to talk to you about the project that I assigned at the team meeting. It has come to my attention that you did not work on it this week. I am not sure why, but I believe that by not speaking to me first it creates a problem for both me as a leader and for the other members of the team. Can we talk about this?" STOP TALKING. (Be prepared to listen to him.)

Depending on how the conversation goes, you may need to more clearly establish expectations for the future.

Poor Performance: Website Willy

Imagine you have a new website designer. Website Willy is creative, personable and his final product is excellent. However, the issue is that he rarely does what he says he is going to do within the time frame in which he says he is going to do it. To make a long story short, Website Willy's lack of timely follow-through is driving you crazy. Your judgmental inside voice is ranting, "Willy is overcommitted and super-disorganized. Seriously, does he think he lives on a planet where deadlines don't matter? How self-absorbed do you have to be to think that time actually stands still for you? I don't know how he copes in the *real* world - it certainly doesn't seem like he's coping very well at work!"

Before you let your inside voice totally take control, remind yourself to stick with the cold, hard facts. It *is* true that Website Willy told you that he can deliver certain elements of the website within a certain time frame and that he has not done what he had promised on a number of occasions. The problem is that you are wasting time following up with him on the changes that you have requested. The bigger concern is the new website material is delayed, which could potentially undermine your credibility with your clients. These are the facts in three sentences and you have correctly identified the problem these facts are causing. Now, what could you say to Willy?

"Willy, I want to talk to you about the website development. I have been frustrated lately as there have been a number of occasions in the last month in which you promised certain components of the website and they have not been done. I believe these have a negative impact on the professionalism of my website. I am also starting to feel like your mother nagging you. I know I am not enjoying it and I suspect you aren't either! Can we talk about this?" STOP TALKING. (Time to hear him out.)

Bad Behavior: Hello Again, Lazy Linda!

Let's go back and talk to Linda, your coworker who has not been getting her reports done on time. Linda has just informed you that she is sadly too darn busy to do her portion of the assigned report, which is due to be presented in only a few days. You are fuming. "No time, my butt!" you say to yourself. "This is just like her. She had time to take a long lunch with her new boyfriend, but no time to do her work. Really!"

Your grumbly inside voice aside, you *have* heard Linda whispering "sweet nothings" on her cell phone and seen her texting like a fiend all week. This is not the first time this has happened; in fact it is a bit of a pattern, especially when there is a new man in her life. So what do you do? You go ahead and finish the report yourself like you have done many times before.

What is the underlying issue, here? I am sorry to say that you are a part of the problem. Linda has learned that if she does not step up to the plate, you will bail her out. Although you probably feel helpless each time this issue presents itself, you *do* have control over your actions. The other issue is that Linda did not do her assigned section of the report. She has told you she has no time to do it and yet you have seen with your own eyes what she does during work hours. When having the conversation, you may want to let Linda know that you are feeling frustrated and resentful about her not doing her assigned portion of the report. Here is one way you could word this tough conversation:

> "Linda, I've noticed a pattern when we work together on reports. On several occasions, including this week, you have told me you are too busy to provide the input for your part of the report. I am frustrated because I see you spending time on personal matters and I end up doing the entire job because I don't want our group to look bad. I am worried if we don't figure out a way to handle this going forward, I am going to become more resentful and it is going to affect our working relationship." STOP TALKING. (Silence is powerful.)

Whew! That is a good one to have over with! Now Linda knows her patterns at work are an issue. We have to let people know how their behavior affects us if there is to be any hope that things will change. (A note of caution: don't expect instant results. Our messages sometimes need space to sink in.)

But I Have No Time!

Taking the time to separate fact from fiction before you launch into a conversation that you anticipate will be difficult may seem like a waste of time, especially for those of you with Type A personalities (trust me, I can relate). Sometimes problems seem so obvious that you are indignant at the thought of squandering even more of your time and energy clarifying the facts, especially after all the time and energy you have already spent worrying about the issue at hand.

"Before anything else, preparation is the key to success."

- Alexander Graham Bell

Rest assured that the preparation you do upfront *is* worthwhile; not only will it help you to clarify what is at stake and what the issues are, it will also ensure you don't blurt out the first thing that comes to mind. As I tell my son and my nephew (who bicker like siblings), relationships cannot always be mended with "I'm sorry," so spend the time to be clear on whether this is a conversation you need to have and why.

Top Tools to Recall: Nailing Down the Real Issue

- ✔ Until you can identify what the issue or problem is, you cannot address it. Until you address it you cannot solve it.
- ✔ Discovering the real issue or problem requires you to separate fact from fiction.
- ✔ Negotiating with your "inside voice" and having a mental dump of your assumptions, beliefs and judgments will help you get to the facts - and you may feel lighter too!
- ✔ Get specific: Ask yourself what the other person is doing or not doing (just the facts) that is causing a problem for you or others. Summarize for yourself in three sentences or less.

Until now, you have been a detective examining the cold, hard evidence. With the information you have gathered you have distilled the issue or problem into three factual sentences or less. You have dealt with your inside voice to quiet the constant chattering by questioning what you had filed away as "very important and true information" (a.k.a. your beliefs, assumptions and judgments). You may have even had a mental dump.

The next step is to clarify your goal for the conversation - what you are actually hoping to achieve by having this talk. Your goal will be your guiding light and something you will want to revisit while you are having the conversation, if and when things start to heat up.

Tame the Elephant in the Office

(in 4 pretty easy steps)

Step 1: Prepare to Talk

Get clear about what the real issue is and write it down in three sentences or less. Then determine what your ultimate goal is for the conversation. Be realistic.

Step 2: Design and Deliver Your "ABC Message"

What do you say and how do you say it? It's as easy as "ABC:" make it Accurate, Brief and Clear. Don't waste your time dancing around the issue; be honest and give people the "straight goods" in a way that is respectful and nonjudgmental.

Step 3: Stop Talking and Start Listening

Once you have delivered your ABC message, listen without interruption to hear the other person out. This may be your toughest challenge, but it is essential to keep the conversation on track... and it is easier than you think!

Step 4: Respond Powerfully

This is your opportunity to respond (not react) and clarify in a way that is confident, concise and clear. No excuses. No justifications. No blame.

Chapter 4:

Hammer Out Your Goal

Chapter highlights:

- ❑ *What are you hoping to accomplish by having this conversation?*
- ❑ *Focus on what you can achieve: Is your goal realistic?*
- ❑ *Have a backup plan if the conversation goes sour or you don't get cooperation from the other person.*

Before you open your mouth to talk to someone, it is absolutely essential that you ask yourself what you are hoping to achieve in having this conversation; in other words, what is your goal? You need to focus on what you *can* do: something that is realistic, within your control and productive. You also need to think about having a plan if the conversation goes sideways or you do not get cooperation from the other person. Ask yourself, "What is the bottom line here? What can I live with?"

The reality is that many of us go into difficult conversations without really knowing what we want to get out of it or what we will do if we hit the ditch (as we inevitably do from time to time). We just know we need to say something because we are upset, irritated or frustrated. We think about what we want the other

"You can't hit a home run unless you step up to the plate. You can't catch a fish unless you put your line in the water. You can't reach your goals if you don't try."
- Kathy Seligman[9]

person to do and we think about how we want them to change. We are so busy worrying about the other person that we really don't pay enough attention to what it is that *we* really want to gain from having the talk in the first place. If we don't truly, clearly know what it is that we want, then talking to the other person is pointless because there cannot be a clear and productive direction. The conversation rambles along and we say to ourselves, "How did we end up talking about *this*?" or "Where did things go so terribly wrong?" I have been there and done that too many times. Remember how Alice fell down the rabbit hole because she wandered around without any direction? Having clarity about your goals can help you to steer clear of rabbit holes, ditches, land mines... you get the idea.

Clarify a Productive Goal

If the intent of your conversation is to be respectful and honest, then you are on the right track to a productive goal. If you are having the talk for the right reasons - and you are prepared and willing to be open and curious about the other person - then chances are increased that the conversation will turn out how you want it to. (My friend Scottie from this book's introduction has proven it to me time and again.) Be warned that if you are still fuming about your most recent altercation at the office, you may be tempted to make the intent of your conversation less than honorable, say by putting the offending person down or attempting to upset the person in retaliation for how upset you have been. I am here to tell you that as long as your intent is to simply vent your anger, you will never be able to truly get what you want out of a difficult conversation. To make real, genuine progress, you need to focus on what you *can* achieve, something that is doable, productive and within your control.

And what is that, exactly? Well, you can choose what you communicate and how you communicate it. If you choose wisely, that should help get the ball rolling in the right direction. Unfortunately, you cannot change someone else's behavior, attitudes or reactions - but perhaps you have figured that out already. If you try to change people (as I regrettably have, more times than I'd like to admit), I guarantee you are going to hit a brick wall eventually. People only change when they want to and they are more likely to make changes if they feel that we have treated them respectfully.

The Backup Plan

Part of goal setting is creating a backup plan in case the conversation goes sour or your message goes in one ear and out the other. Your backup plan will give you the best chance of having a successful conversation. You cannot control how someone else is going to react or behave as a result of your conversation, but having a backup plan in place will give you the confidence you need to stay the course if things become challenging. If you do not get cooperation from the other person or if things continue to go downhill, then the backup plan is your trump card. It allows you to have the conversation with the knowledge that you are not dependent on the other person's cooperation, which makes you far less likely to come across as desperate, whiny or aggressive.

Helpful Hint: The Key to Creating Your Backup Plan

Ensure that:

1. Your backup plan does not rely on the other person's cooperation; *and*
2. Your backup plan is something you can live with. Be honest with yourself here!

If, during the conversation, you chose to reveal your backup plan to the other person, be prepared to follow through with it. Take a look at the following cautionary tale:

You have just emphatically told your client that there are going to be no more special requests or rush orders, only to have a call from them the following day asking you to squeeze in one more rush order. They promise that this is the last time (but haven't you heard that before?) and you predictably cave after some begging, taking on their crisis as your own. Uh oh - you have just reinforced that your "no" is not really a "no;" in fact it sounds an awful lot like a big fat "yes!" If this is the pattern you set for yourself, you are ultimately never going to get what you want out of your tough conversations because you are undermining yourself by not committing to your backup plan.

The key to having a solid backup plan is to make sure it is something that you absolutely 100% can follow through on without waffling. This must be true whether you tell the other person your plan or not. In the example we just looked at with the begging customer, your backup plan might be to follow your standard operating procedure of three days to process an order. To implement your backup plan, you must calmly and confidently make your decisions clear to your customer with an "ABC message" (more on ABC messages in step two of "Taming the Elephant in the Office," starting in chapter six).

Here is one way you might reinforce your backup plan:

> "You know that I value you as a client and I want to provide the best possible service. The way I can do that and ensure efficiency and fairness for all of my clients is by guaranteeing a three-day turnaround time on all orders. I can have this order to you within three days." STOP TALKING. (If you don't, you will inevitably shoot yourself in the foot.)

Let's look at some work situations to see how a clear, productive goal and a realistic backup plan for the conversation will help things stay focused.

Delivering Sensitive News: Bad Breath Betty

Your colleague, Betty, has terrible breath. You work together on projects and the smell is really bothering you. You offer her gum constantly. You even bought mouthwash and put it on your desk as part of an ingenious plan: you use the mouthwash regularly and make sure to tell Betty about its amazing effectiveness and delicious flavor, in hopes she will pick up on your clues. Sadly, your less-than-subtle hints have not worked.

"Nothing will ever be attempted if all possible objections must first be overcome."

- Samuel Johnson

Okay, so what is the problem? You have noticed that Betty has bad breath. Your goal for the conversation is to sensitively let her know (in a caring but honest way) that you have noticed her bad breath because you believe she deserves to know and also because you desperately crave a less smelly coworker. Do you need a backup plan? That depends. If Betty is your secretary and she is dealing with the public, you might need a backup plan, such as moving her into the back part of the office, if things don't improve. If she is a colleague then you likely just want to let her know about her bad breath. In this case, a backup plan is not needed because you do not have any reasonable means of motivating Betty to correct her bad breath issue beyond letting her know it is unpleasant.

How can you say something to Betty?

> "Betty, I have something to say and it is a bit awkward. I have noticed the last few times we have met that you have had bad breath. I know if it were me, I would want someone to tell me." STOP TALKING. (Saying anything more will just prolong the pain.)

Delivering Bad or Sad News: Beloved Boss

One of the most difficult conversations I had was telling one of my beloved bosses that I was leaving the firm and moving to Los Angeles to follow my soon-to-be hubby and his career. My hubby kept asking, "Have you told him yet?" I kept putting off the conversation until I felt like I was getting an ulcer. Why was it so difficult to have this conversation? Well, I loved my job and I didn't want to let my boss and my coworkers down. Also, I didn't want to be seen as just another woman who left a great job for a man. I really viewed myself as a career woman and I was not going to sell out for a man or motherhood (I was a naïve 20-something). The internal conflict was killing me. What made delivering this message so tricky was my own identity crisis about what leaving really said about me and what it meant to me. The goal was very clear: tell my boss I was leaving. I did also want to let him know that it had been a difficult decision and I would really miss him and the rest of the team.

Here was my message to him:

> "I don't know how to say this, so I am just going to blurt it out: I am leaving the firm as I have decided to follow my fiancé to Los Angeles where he is pursuing fellowship training. This is one of the most difficult decisions I have had to make. I am really going to miss this place."

Then I followed my own advice and simply stopped talking. Otherwise, I may have agreed to something I didn't want to do - like work remotely or stay on for longer than I wanted to help train a replacement.

Dealing With Rude or Disrespectful Behavior: Colorful Cal

Imagine your boss, Cal, loves to use colorful and what you regard to be inappropriate language. Your goal in talking to him may be just to let him know that when he uses this kind of language, you feel uncomfortable. It is about letting him know the impact of his behavior on you. It might be that simple - nothing more, nothing less. It is really about asserting yourself and speaking your mind without necessarily expecting anything concrete in return. If his behavior is really upsetting to you and you don't see any improvement, your backup plan may be to leave meetings when he starts using language that makes you uncomfortable or, in the extreme, you could go to human resources and ask to be transferred to a different department. It is unlikely in this first conversation that you would say anything to Cal about your backup plan. Having a backup plan is really about giving you peace of mind so you don't avoid having an awkward conversation, as opposed to using it to coerce or threaten someone into changing (which could definitely backfire, especially with your boss).

Here is something you might say:

> "Cal, I don't want to be difficult, but I wanted to let you know that I feel uncomfortable when you swear in our meetings. I would appreciate it if you did not use profanities in front of me." STOP TALKING. (Remember that brevity is powerful.)

Dealing With Poor Performance: One-Task Tammy

Imagine you have inherited an employee who has been in her job a long time and yet is only able to perform the most basic functions. Her inability to do everything her job entails has never been properly addressed. You know this is affecting the rest of the team because they have been (reluctantly) picking up the slack. Now resentment is building as workloads increase. Your goal in talking to Tammy is to let her know your expectation that she must be able to do all of her job functions. You are concerned that you may be trying to put a Band-Aid on a hemorrhage, but you feel she at least deserves a chance. You decide you are willing to offer her retraining with a concrete action plan, if she thinks that will help, or you can give her the option to be transferred to a more junior position in the mailroom. Your backup plan may be ultimately to demote her.

Here's what you might say to Tammy:

> "Tammy, I want to let you know that my expectations going forward are that you are able to do all parts of this job. I am willing to arrange some retraining with a concrete plan for follow-up, or I can offer you a position in the mailroom. The decision of what you would like to do is yours. Do you have any thoughts or questions about this?" STOP TALKING. (You may undermine your message if you keep yacking.)

Saying No: Snow Day Sue

You work downtown and some employees commute long distances. One day it begins to snow heavily; predictably, traffic is snarled and public transportation is at a standstill. You advise your staff that those who need to leave early can do so, but the office will remain open. Several commuters ask to leave an hour or two early, including Sue, whom you know lives close to the office and walks to work every day. You had anticipated this request; it wouldn't be the first time that Sue had used an inappropriate excuse to get out of work early. (Oops, quiet that inside voice!)

As far as your goal for the conversation, you are quite clear that you want to tell Sue that no, she can't leave work early. Your backup plan is to offer her unpaid time off if she insists on leaving early. Ultimately, having this backup plan gives you the strength to stand firm, even under her anticipated opposition.

How might you say no to Snow Day Sue?

> "Sue, I need you to be one of the team that stays in the office until the end of the day. If you won't stay, then I will be asking you to take the time off without pay."
> STOP TALKING. (There is nothing more to say.)

Summing Up

A key to goal setting is to think through what you will do if the conversation goes sour or if you do not get cooperation from the other person. This will help you to formulate a solid backup plan. Remember that a backup plan isn't a backup plan unless you really mean to follow through. Do not threaten to quit, report somebody, fire somebody or anything else unless you really would do it. Make sure you can live with the consequences of your backup plan. Your credibility and your self-esteem are on the line; plus, if you reveal a backup plan you really don't intend to put into action, you may end up backing yourself into a corner or putting yourself in an otherwise extremely difficult situation.

Top Tools to Recall: Hammering Out Your Goal

- ✔ Your goal should be doable, productive and something that is within your control.
- ✔ Have a backup plan if the conversation bottoms out; it will give you the courage to speak up with confidence.
- ✔ Your backup plan should not be dependent on the other person's cooperation.

Sometimes, when we are thinking about our primary goal for a difficult conversation, what we really want to do is control the other person or the outcome, somehow force that person to change, or criticize, guilt or shame the other person in retaliation for our own hurt feelings. Let's be honest here: if everyone would just agree with us or if no one's feelings were on the line, these conversations would really not be that tough!

"Without goals and plans to reach them, you are like a ship that has set sail with no destination."

\- Fitzhugh Dodson[10]

There is a real danger that you may secretly (or even unconsciously) have an unproductive goal for your difficult conversation, which will pretty much guarantee that things will go badly. Having unproductive goals only prevents us from getting what we really need from our tough talks. In the next chapter, we will be uncovering some of the potential pitfalls of unproductive goals and how you can sidestep them.

Tame the Elephant in the Office
(in 4 pretty easy steps)

Step 1: Prepare to Talk

Get clear about what the real issue is and write it down in three sentences or less. Then determine what your ultimate goal is for the conversation. Be realistic.

Step 2: Design and Deliver Your "ABC Message"

What do you say and how do you say it? It's as easy as "ABC:" make it Accurate, Brief and Clear. Don't waste your time dancing around the issue; be honest and give people the "straight goods" in a way that is respectful and nonjudgmental.

Step 3: Stop Talking and Start Listening

Once you have delivered your ABC message, listen without interruption to hear the other person out. This may be your toughest challenge, but it is essential to keep the conversation on track... and it is easier than you think!

Step 4: Respond Powerfully

This is your opportunity to respond (not react) and clarify in a way that is confident, concise and clear. No excuses. No justifications. No blame.

Chapter 5:

Resist the Temptation

Chapter highlights:

- ☐ *Lose the urge to control or change the other person.*
- ☐ *Forget trying to prove that you are "right."*
- ☐ *Resist the desire to sneakily insult or undermine the other person.*
- ☐ *Let go of any expectations of avoiding a negative reaction to your tough conversation.*

"What makes resisting temptation difficult for many people is they don't want to discourage it completely."

- Franklin P. Jones[11]

One of the biggest pitfalls we tumble into in our tough talks is when there is a disconnect between what we say we want to get out of the conversation and what we secretly hope to achieve. Remember a true goal should be realistic, honest and productive. If you are trying to control the other person, make them change, prove you are right, prevent them from having a negative reaction, make a sneaky dig (or two) or get back at them, let me tell you right now that these are not the kinds of goals that will lead to success. This is your desire for control, your hurt feelings or your wounded ego taking over the situation. I know because I am speaking from experience. It will be obvious if you have made any of the above your "real goals" for the conversation; respect will vanish and things will go sideways, just what you had originally feared and desperately wanted to avoid.

Lose the Urge to Control the Other Person

Control is good in some parts of your life (pantyhose, Spandex, your crazy impulses...). However, when your goal is to try to control others by changing them, making them "see the light," delivering ultimatums or trying to prevent them from being upset, your conversation is doomed. There are a few truths when it comes to these tough talks and I remind myself about them on a regular basis:

1. *You can't control someone else's reaction.*

Often when you go into these conversations, the last thing you want to do is hurt or upset the other person. However, you cannot make "being nice" your goal because it will inevitably interfere with your ability to communicate in a straightforward and honest way. You end up doctoring your message as you try to cushion the blow and control the other person's reactions. You hope the other person will smile and be happy and not see you as an unkind, petty or difficult person. When you are concern yourself with preserving your own image as a nice and reasonable person, chances are you aren't communicating in a clear and honest way.

Think of the last time you didn't get a job or you weren't chosen for a project. The person starts in with a big, long song and dance about how great you are, how you are just so amazing and that the decision, well, it really wasn't personal. Doesn't it just feel so insincere? When people spin stories, my B.S. meter goes off big time and I feel that they are more concerned with preserving their image as a nice person and/or trying to prevent me from being upset than with being honest and straight with me. I lose respect for them. The lesson is not to try to cushion the blow or prevent the other person from getting upset because it will only aggravate him or her more. People have pretty sensitive B.S. meters and I promise you, they will catch on - and instead of looking like "the nice guy," which was the reason you started altering your message in the first place, you end up looking worse than if you had just been straightforward from the start.

Let's take a specific workplace example of when we may be tempted to try to prevent the other person from having a negative emotional reaction:

Imagine you are a manager who needs to tell your hardworking employee, Gail, that despite your assurances and her outstanding performance reviews, she actually did not get the promotion that she was expecting. Why? Because someone from head office with seniority decided to move to your region and she wants the job. It is the right decision for the organization, but you are worried that Gail will be devastated. Now, you tell yourself that the decision was out of your control (and it really was); however, you still had led Gail to believe that she was a shoo-in for the job. You feel sick about it and you need to tell her. You are worried that she might start crying. She has done that before and it makes you squirm - so you try to prevent her from being upset and you say:

"Gail, you know that I think you are fabulous and you are doing an amazing job. Well, there is no easy way to tell you this: Lisa from head office has decided to move to our region and, given her experience and seniority, she wants to take the position you were applying for. I had no way of knowing that this would happen and it is really out of my control. I know that there will be many opportunities for somebody with your talent. Maybe we can work on your performance plan and goal setting so that you will be ready when more opportunities come. I just think you are so great. To be honest I don't think there is any reason to be upset; I bet something even better is just around the corner!"

Ugh! Now, Gail may be a crier, but she's no dummy and this message is not the straight goods. Your feeble attempt to preserve your image as "the good guy" will shine through and all it does is undermine your relationship with Gail. The message just doesn't come across as genuine. By contrast, the following message does a better job at delivering a tough message:

> "Gail, there is no easy way to say this. You did not get the promotion you were hoping for. Lisa from head office has decided to move to our region and she has been given the position. I had no idea that this was a possibility. I apologize. This must be tough news."
> STOP TALKING. (Let the message sink in.)

You can talk about Gail's future opportunities at a later time. Right now she just needs to process the the news, news that really can't be sugar coated - so it is best not to try.

2. *You can't change anyone.*

If your goal is to make the other person change, forget it. People will only change when and if they want to. If they are told something is wrong with them, they dig their heels in and go on the defensive immediately. Think about the last time someone tried to make *you* change: What was your reaction? Did you accept the criticism with open arms or put up a fight (inwardly if not outwardly)? Probably, you were not overly accommodating. It simply is not realistic to expect the target of your discontent to roll over and change just because you asked. You will get better results with a more realistic approach.

Just to be clear here: knowing you cannot change somebody does not mean that you have to put up with poor behavior or performance. It means that you have to let people know your concerns as well as your expectations, and then leave it up to them to decide what they do with the information. You are coming from the perspective of "they deserve to know" and, while you can't control anyone, you *can* control how you deliver the message and develop a backup plan for if the conversation goes sour or you don't get any cooperation from the other person.

Here is a pretty ubiquitous scenario: Imagine that your disorganized boss, Dennis, loves to hold impromptu meetings at the end of the day, which inevitably makes you miss your last connecting bus home. Naturally, there are times when we all wish we could change our boss and secretly, your goal may be that Dennis magically transforms into a more organized, more thoughtful boss - but we know it's not going to happen, right?

Instead of this:

> "Dennis, you are a great boss and I love working with you. I just wish that you would be a little more organized; it would be really helpful to me. I don't mind doing the extra work but if you could just think about what has to get done earlier in the day, that would really be great."

Don't expect a lot of change if you say something like this because you haven't been clear about your expectations or concerns regarding Dennis' disorganization. What *is* in your control is to share the impact of his actions on you and inform him of your plans.

Try saying this instead:

> "Dennis, I wanted to let you know that I will be leaving the office no later than 5:00pm in order to catch my last connecting bus home. If you would like to have a meeting with me, it needs to be concluded by that time as I am no longer able to stay late." STOP TALKING (or you risk sabotaging your message).

Now, you can't force Dennis to see things your way, but the key here is that when you communicate a boundary or expectation, it is absolutely essential that you follow through on it. Otherwise, the impact of your conversation will get thrown out the window.

3. *Putting someone down is not the right tack.*

I worked on an interesting case many years ago under the tutelage of a senior lawyer I will call "Harv the Humiliator." I was a young lawyer and still learning, but I worked hard, was very diligent and took my work very seriously. As we approached the trial date, we entered into settlement negotiations, as is often the case, and eventually the case settled out of court. As the junior lawyer on the file (a.k.a. the gopher), I did all of the research and other uninteresting tasks. After the case settled, Harv called me into his office for a debrief and started to question me on my research for the case. To my embarrassment, the conversation went something like this:

> *Harv:* Diane, you did the research on the case, right?
>
> *Me:* Yes.
>
> *My Inside Voice:* Uh oh, what the heck is going on here? Why would he even ask me a question like that?
>
> *Harv:* Can you tell me if you looked at all of the relevant cases?
>
> *Me:* Yes, I did.
>
> *My Inside Voice:* Did I do something wrong? Why is he doing this now?
>
> *Harv:* I can assume you looked up cases with similar injuries to this complainant. Is that correct?
>
> *Me:* Yes.
>
> *My Inside Voice:* Oh man, what did I miss? This does not sound good!

Harv then pulled out a book of cases from his shelf, flipped to a previously marked page and said, "Did you happen to find *this* case, Diane?"

By this point, my face was all red and hot; I was so scrambled that I quickly looked over the pages in front of me and said quietly, "I don't think so."

My inside voice was screaming, "What a jerk! This case isn't relevant anyway!" Of course, I was feeling defensive because he had just questioned my competence big time.

Then Harv said, "Well, opposing counsel thinks this is an important case. It should have been included in your research, if you had managed to find it." Just like that, I was dismissed like a poorly prepared school girl.

I was humiliated and talked to anyone who would listen about how misguided, arrogant and condescending Harv was. I dug my heels in about how wrong he was and, of course, how right I was. My research was sound; he didn't have his facts straight. I reviewed the case and it was not relevant. The other lawyer was the one who messed up, not me! The result? I learned nothing and Harv was now "difficult" in my books.

As I reflect back many years later, I think maybe Harv had some valid concerns about how I had approached my research. The problem was how he broached it. If his goal for the conversation was to humiliate me, then he succeeded. If his goal was to have me spend time (he was paying me after all) to complain about him behind his back, then he definitely succeeded there! If his goal was to find out how I went about my research to identify gaps in my process and give me an opportunity to learn for the future, then he failed miserably.

If I Had a Do-Over...

Okay, we can't change others. We can only change ourselves and that, my friends, is no easy task. I remind myself that I may see myself with lots of grey hair before I see other people change so, if I want action, I need to take action myself. At that earlier stage in my life and my career, I chose the "avoid-complain" option, which was not productive for anyone involved, especially since I cared a lot about my reputation as a conscientious worker. Too bad I didn't know about the two-minute whine rule back then because, as you can easily guess, I did a lot of whining but nothing was actually resolved.

So, what could I have done? After the meeting, I should have taken a bit of time to cool off and engage in a two-minute whine with a buddy. (Remember, two minutes of complaining and then develop an action plan to deal with the issue.) Then I should have prepared myself for a conversation with Harv to let him know how his behavior had affected me. Step one: ignore my whining inside voice nattering away about his arrogance and rudeness. Step two: stifle my assumptions, "hot" language and judgments about my boss because they certainly wouldn't improve our working relationship. Step three: let him know how his behavior had affected me. My goals in talking to him could have been to let him know (a) that I was embarrassed by how he had spoken to me about my work on the file and (b) that I care about doing a good job and take concerns or criticisms about my work seriously.

"When you can't change the direction of the wind, adjust your sails."

- H. Jackson Brown Jr.[12]

I could have said something like this:

> "I was wondering if we could talk about the meeting we had the other day. When you called me into your office, asked me a number of questions about my research and then pulled the case off the shelf and asked me if I had seen it, I was taken aback. I had the sense that you thought I really messed up. I am not sure what your intentions were, but I felt humiliated. I need you to know that I take my work seriously and I have a lot of pride in what I do. Could we talk about any suggestions you have about how I should be going about my research to make sure that I am doing what is necessary? STOP TALKING (time to listen).

Later I could have stated my views on the relevance of the case. This was not the time; doing so would have only gotten Harv's back up.

The bottom line: If your "real goal" is an unproductive one, such as putting someone down or trying to humiliate them, your conversation will inevitably backfire. Also keep in mind that it does not matter which side of the conflict you are on; you have more power than you think and you can use the conversation tools in this book to get what you need in the workplace. Don't wait for others to change. Take charge and don't miss an opportunity to "clear the air." Straightforward and honest is always best.

Top Tools to Recall: Resisting Unproductive Goals

- ✔ If your goal is to change someone, prove you are right, make them "see the light," prevent them from being upset, preserve your own image or make a dig, the conversation is not going to go well.

- ✔ Make sure that your goal is actually productive and not about protecting your own ego or someone else's.

- ✔ Even if you stifle unproductive goals for a time, they will eventually leak out in your body language or with some unkind quip and it will backfire! Have an honest talk with yourself so that you can let go of any hidden agendas and unproductive goals that risk sabotaging your real goal for your tough talk.

Congratulations! Now you know what you need to do to prepare for a tough conversation: you have nailed down the issue and hammered out your goal. You have learned that avoiding the conversation will just create stress and sleepless nights, but not give you an outcome you actually want.

All right, so you are determined to have this conversation, but you are wondering, "Yeah, but *how* am I actually going to *say* it?" Coming up next are some very important tools to give you the confidence you need. If fear is what has been holding you back, get ready to lose that excuse, too! You are about to empower yourself to communicate with clarity. Let's go!

Tame the Elephant in the Office (in 4 pretty easy steps)

Step 1: Prepare to Talk

Get clear about what the real issue is and write it down in three sentences or less. Then determine what your ultimate goal is for the conversation. Be realistic.

Step 2: Design and Deliver Your "ABC Message"

What do you say and how do you say it? It's as easy as "ABC:" make it Accurate, Brief and Clear. Don't waste your time dancing around the issue; be honest and give people the "straight goods" in a way that is respectful and nonjudgmental.

Step 3: Stop Talking and Start Listening

Once you have delivered your ABC message, listen without interruption to hear the other person out. This may be your toughest challenge, but it is essential to keep the conversation on track... and it is easier than you think!

Step 4: Respond Powerfully

This is your opportunity to respond (not react) and clarify in a way that is confident, concise and clear. No excuses. No justifications. No blame.

Step 2:

Design and Deliver Your "ABC Message"

Chapter 6: Designing Your ABC Message

Chapter 7: Delivering Your ABC Message

Chapter 6:

Designing Your ABC Message

Chapter highlights:

- ☐ *Accurate: Stick to the facts, use "I" statements and avoid "hot," judgmental language.*
- ☐ *Brief: Less is more - deliver your message in 30 seconds or less.*
- ☐ *Clear: Get straight to the heart of the matter.*

"I am prepared to go anywhere, provided it be forward."

- David Livingstone[13]

Now we are getting to the meat and potatoes of the book - creating the right message. You want to craft messages that are accurate, brief and clear - your ABC message - and those messages should describe what you saw, heard and experienced. It is about giving people the straight goods in a way that is respectful and nonjudgmental. Remember how Scottie talked to me about my behavior when I was getting a laugh at someone else's expense? He didn't say, "Diane, you are so rude!" or "Diane, I can't believe how disrespectful you are," or "Diane, you are totally out of line." Instead he said that *he* was uncomfortable with what I had said. There is a big difference because he made his message about him rather than it being about criticizing me.

The other element of a good ABC message is that people would rather have the straight goods than have you "spin" things or avoid issues altogether. They also want to hear your message *now*, not a year from now when memories have faded. They do not want to try and interpret it or figure out what your point is because it was buried in the middle of a long-winded and confusing speech. There is nothing worse for the other person than expecting the ax to fall and then, by the end of your message, not even being sure of what you were trying to say.

A Little Inspiration

When I first started trying to improve my communication skills, I felt really apprehensive and uncomfortable, so I wrote down a formula for my messages that Scottie had shared with me.[14] It went like this:

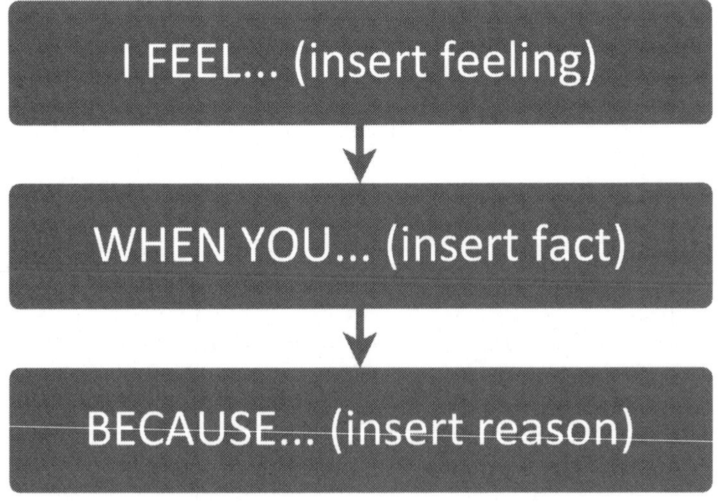

I shared this formula with my family and colleagues and soon we were all practicing Scottie's formula on each other. The only problem was that for me it went something like this: *I felt* embarrassed (check!) *when you* told me my work was below standard (check!) *because* you are an arrogant know-it-all who didn't take the time to appreciate my hard work (oops!). You can see where this went off the rails: the "because" was followed by judgment or blame. Through much trial and error, I have learned to be able to deliver my message genuinely without a formula in hand because, let's face it, no formula works for every situation (although it can certainly help you get started). I take ownership of the statements I make and I do not assume bad intentions on the part of the other person (at least on my good days!). Remember to resist the temptation to put the other person down; your results will always be better when you take the high road.

Now I can say:

> "I felt embarrassed when you told me my report was below standard because I take pride in my work and it is important to me that it is well done. Can we talk about what was missing from your perspective?"

Much better! In fact, I give myself a great big gold star for that message! The difference is that I am taking ownership of my reason ("I take pride in my work") versus blaming the other person for my embarrassment ("you are an arrogant know-it-all"). And I'm telling you, if there is hope for me, there is hope for everyone! Crafting your message does not have to feel impossible, once you know your "ABCs."

Nuts and Bolts of the ABC Method

"A" is for "Accurate"

Messages should be accurate. That means no exaggeration! You are not writing a thriller, creating a soap opera or developing a Broadway play. Your real life drama has all of the excitement you need, trust me. Be absolutely clear in your own mind what so-called "facts" and feelings are associated with your subjective, judgmental and temperamental inside voice. You have already had this discussion once with that nattering voice in your head when you identified the real issue, so be careful not to let your inside voice become your outside voice when it comes time to actually speak to the other person.

Here is your "A" toolkit:

1. Stick to the facts.

Remember your assumptions, interpretations and judgments are not facts, even if everyone agrees with you. You have to negotiate with your judgmental, know-it-all inside voice so you can separate fact from fiction. I love this example that I use in my workshops: I ask the group, "Is it a fact that Roger Federer is a great tennis player?" The answer is almost always a resounding "yes" - but then again, what does "great" mean anyway? A factual statement is that Roger Federer has won 17 Grand Slams (at least that was the case when I wrote this book), but "great" is a subjective description of Roger Federer, as opposed to being a true fact.

We love to state our opinions as facts, but saying something is a fact does not make it so, even if lots of people agree with us. Factual statements may sound like this:

- ✔ Jack arrived between five and ten minutes late for our last three meetings (as opposed to: "Jack must need a new watch because he is *never* on time").
- ✔ Jennifer did not meet service standards this week (instead of: "Jennifer must not care about her clients at all; she always keeps them waiting").
- ✔ Suzy has called in sick 10 times this month (versus: "Gee, Suzy is ill again? What a surprise! She obviously does not take her job very seriously").

During one of my workshops, a participant was preparing for a tough conversation. She was trying to look at the facts and told me, "Okay, the fact is that he is difficult." She was genuinely convinced that this was an accurate and factual statement. But was it? Not at all. Statements like these are subjective and don't get to the heart of the matter.

I asked her, "What did this person actually do that led you to the conclusion that he is difficult?"

She was emphatic and repeated, "He is just difficult and everyone knows it." Now, in her mind, she had backed up that "fact" with the evidence that "everyone knows it," which gave her confidence that she was right and I just didn't get it. But how can she have a productive conversation when the only "fact" she can offer is going to get this guy's back up?

So what would be a statement based on fact? How about: "I find it very difficult to work with John because he often changes his mind about the direction on the project, for example last week when he..." Now that deserves a gold star!

2. Use "I" statements whenever possible.

"I think," "I am," "I want," "I believe," "I need" and "I feel" can all make good starts to great "I" statements. Here are a few examples for you:

- ✔ *I think* it is important for everyone to have an opportunity to be heard. I would like to give James the opportunity to finish sharing his ideas.

- ✔ *I am* concerned about taking that position with the client.

- ✔ *I want* everyone to present at the upcoming conference.

- ✔ *I believe* we need to look at some other options here to make the best and most informed decision.

- ✔ *I need* to have everyone on board with this change initiative.

- ✔ *I felt* upset when you told Tom about our disagreement. I thought that the matter was private.

Using "I" statements allows you to share your opinions and feelings, but it is important that you use "I" statements responsibly. We often say "I feel" in broad sweeping statements that really have nothing to do with feelings.

For example:

- ✗ I feel it is inappropriate to send text messages in meetings.
- ✗ I feel like you don't care about my development in my role as supervisor.
- ✗ I feel you are a jerk.
- ✗ I feel you don't appreciate anything I do for you.

Statements such as these are assumptions and judgments hidden in "I" statements. They are also full of judgmental language and assume negative intentions on the part of others. These kinds of comments will certainly not get you where you want to go and may even raise a critical eyebrow or two if they slip out in front of other people.

If you use the phrase "I feel," make sure that a real feeling follows. Our repertoire for critical, judgmental and blaming language is generally much more developed and refined than our vocabulary of feelings. You may have to work at finding "feeling" language beyond the typical angry, upset, hurt, happy variety. One way to avoid using "I feel" inappropriately is to replace it with "I am," such as "I am concerned," "I am annoyed," "I am upset," "I am worried," etc.

3. Put judgmental terms aside because, sadly, they are not facts.

Contrast the statements below with the ones that follow.

Instead of this:

- ✗ It is *rude* to gossip.
- ✗ It is *inappropriate* to talk about your sex life at work.
- ✗ It is *disrespectful* to be late all the time.
- ✗ Your behavior at the client lunch was *unprofessional.*

...Say this:

- ✓ I am not comfortable talking about Elizabeth when she is not present.
- ✓ I am not comfortable when you talk about your sex life with me.
- ✓ I am frustrated when you arrive late to our brainstorming sessions because it wastes everyone else's time.
- ✓ I am not sure if you are aware that you interrupted the client on a number of occasions at our lunch meeting.

Much of our "hot" and judgmental language relates to how *we* see the world, as opposed to how things actually are. Your worldview may differ from another person's, which is why if you present your worldview as the consummate truth or the "right" way to see things, the other person may feel like you are questioning his or her values or character. It is only a matter of time before the other person's back is up, which will inevitably send your conversation sideways.

4. Share the impact of his or her actions without assuming bad intentions on the part of the other person.

How can you do that? Take a look at the following sentences:

- ✔ When you text during client briefings, I am concerned it sends the message that you aren't interested in your clients or what we are discussing.

- ✔ When you raised your voice in the meeting yesterday, I noticed that people stopped participating in the discussion. I believe it created tension in the room.

- ✔ I felt embarrassed when you called me a prima donna in front of the staff.

Although it can be tempting, if you assume negative intentions, chances are the other person will respond defensively and fight you tooth and nail. Imagine being on the receiving end of comments like these:

- ✗ It is just like you to speak to me like that. You love to humiliate others to make yourself feel better.

- ✗ If you were more conscientious, you would plan your time more considerately.

- ✗ If you cared about anyone other than yourself, you'd clean up your mess in the lunchroom.

How could you reword these comments so that they could contribute to a more productive conversation?

- ✓ I felt mortified in our meeting when you told me that I never contribute any worthwhile ideas to the team.
- ✓ I would like to talk to you about how you plan your day so we can ensure your productions goals are met.
- ✓ I noticed that you left your dishes on the counter in the staff room. Would you please put your dishes away when you are finished?

5. Skip the blame game.

If you have ever had a child run in from playing in the yard screeching that her big brother just pulled her ponytail, you know how one-sided the blame game can be (or at least sound). Even as adults, we love to childishly blame others for their actions, their behavior and their bad intentions. However, even if there is a kernel of truth in what you are saying, the fact that your message is cloaked in blaming language makes it very unlikely that you will be heard.

Blaming language often starts with the word "you." I am not saying that it is necessary to extricate the word "you" from your vocabulary, but you do need to be careful about how you use that word in order to avoid sounding like you are blaming the other person. Remember, even if you feel like blaming the other person, all you will accomplish by blaming is putting a wall up between the two of you, which will not help you improve your situation in the workplace.

Instead of this:

- ✗ You are *irresponsible*. You promised you would pick me up at the airport and you didn't.
- ✗ You are totally *disorganized*. You left a patient sitting in the waiting room for over an hour. What were you thinking?
- ✗ It's *your fault* that the file was misplaced. You really need to be more on top of things.
- ✗ Why are you so *lazy*? I am sick of picking up your slack.

None of the statements above will lead to a successful conversation or a smooth working relationship. To make sure your message is heard, do your best to avoid blaming language.

...Try saying this:

- ✓ I was disappointed that you were not at the airport to pick me up. Next time, if there is a problem, can you let me know in advance so I can make other arrangements?
- ✓ Let's talk about what kind of plan we can put in place to ensure patients are seen in a timely manner.
- ✓ Files have gone missing three times this week. Can we talk about the system that you are using so we can try to prevent this from happening again?
- ✓ Your last four assignments have been late. Can we talk about this?

6. Let the truth stand and don't exaggerate or embellish it.

Remove these words from your vocabulary as much as you possibly can:

- ✗ *Never* (e.g. "You never pitch in when things get busy.")
- ✗ *Always* (e.g. "You always disappear when difficult people come to the counter.")
- ✗ *Nothing* (e.g. "Nothing is as important to you as that iPhone.")
- ✗ *Everything* (e.g. "You mess everything up," or "Everything you say is ridiculous.")

Each one of these statements is going to lead to unproductive wasted hours because your message has created the perfect conditions for the other person to try to convince you that what you are saying is not valid. Rest assured that the person's memory will be crystal clear about each and every exception to your sweeping generalization. It really is best to avoid the words above if you don't want your talk to go from "tough conversation" to "giant argument."

Instead of this:

- ✗ You never help tidy the waiting room at the end of the day.

...Say this:

- ✓ I have noticed that three times in the last week you have not helped tidy up the waiting area at the end of the day.

Remember that the idea is to address the actual issue without clouding your conversations with blame.

"B" is for "Brief"

"The more you say, the less people remember. The fewer the words, the greater the profit."
- Francois Fenelon[15]

The next part of your ABC message is the "B:" messages need to be brief if we want them to be heard. Remember, you are not writing a novel, you are not an auctioneer and you are not being paid by the word... so there really is no incentive to blather on. We tend to overwhelm people with too much information, which obscures our message, so keep it simple and brief. Less is more.

Deliver a short, powerful message; 30 seconds or less is ideal and if it takes 2 minutes, it is way too long. Being succinct shows that you are confident; plus, the other person is more likely to hear your message if it is not drowned out in a sea of words.

Here is your "B" toolkit:

1. Decide what is most important and leave it at that.

Don't recite a litany of century-old complaints - talk about only one topic or issue. Whenever I am tempted to dredge up old issues, I remind myself of how irritating it is when someone does that to me and that is usually enough for me to zip it (most of the time anyway!). Plus, bringing up age-old issues only invites the other person to do the same, which means your difficult conversation could quickly degenerate into a full-blown war. Be the bigger person and stick to the issue at hand.

If you deal with issues as they arise, rather than letting them build and fester, you won't have to worry about a laundry list of complaints to tackle down the road. Avoiding or delaying important conversations is problematic because when you do finally speak up, you will undoubtedly say way too much.

We don't want our messages to sound like this:

> "Well, Doug, I guess I have some concerns about your performance and your ability to complete assignments on time. The quality of your work is sometimes kind of an issue because you seem to be missing some key steps... but maybe if you made more of an effort to get along with your coworkers..."

I think you are probably getting the picture. I think back to the many performance reviews over my career... you know, those reviews that are held annually and all of a sudden you are expected to remember every little incident over the past year. You have not had feedback until performance review time and you do not even remember the issue that the reviewer is talking about. It happened 10 months earlier and no one said anything then, so how bad could it have been? Maybe they have you confused with somebody else.

My point is that by sticking with what is most important, you will give your conversation focus and avoid getting sidetracked by old issues that do not relate to the issue at hand. If you *do* get caught up on old issues, you risk not being taken seriously and making the other person feel attacked and bombarded, which is only going to undermine your credibility and potentially start a big fight. Choose your most important issue and focus your conversation on that.

2. Avoid lengthy explanations or justifications.

We often think that we need to go on and on to explain our decision or our perspective. You aren't a lawyer (or even if you are); refrain from going on and on like you are making closing remarks in a courtroom. Your job at this moment is to create an accurate, brief and clear message. Cut the baloney and stop trying to create a message that will get the other person to see things from your perspective by using third-party agreement (like: "Stan and Amy and Rebecca *all* agree with me!"), studies (such as: "Research shows that you are more likely to be happier at work if you don't procrastinate") or other reasoning. All this will do is to undermine the power of your message, not to mention it will exhaust the other person and give him or her more points to argue (such as: "Well, Steven and Greg agree with *me*!" or "I'm actually happy at work; I must not be procrastinating as much as you thought!"). Not good.

If you launch yourself into "convince mode," you will only succeed in looking desperate and unsure of yourself. I think we have all been on the receiving end of these types of unending and unbearable conversations. It is far better to state your point with confidence and brevity; you get your message across without going overboard with unimportant details, which can muddy the waters and obscure your message.

"C" is for "Clear"

When your message is clear, it paves the way to a productive conversation. Clear messages are like a perfectly cleaned window: what you see out of them is the real thing. Say what you mean and don't flounder around using important-sounding terms or fake and flowery language. The other person will not appreciate these attempts at softening the bad news and your efforts will backfire.

Also, do not attempt to drop hints instead of having an actual conversation; I'm telling you, those hints will not be caught. People tend to see things as they want them to be, so if you hope to make a real change in the workplace, you have to skip the "subtle clue approach" and tackle the issue with straightforward and clear language. The clearer you are, the more quickly the conversation you have been dreading will be over.

Here is your "C" toolkit:

1. Get straight to the issue.

Avoid trying to bury your message; you're kidding yourself if you think that people don't see through you when you try to hide your issues in less unpleasant topics. When you try to hide your message, the other person is just waiting for the other shoe to drop. All you are doing is prolonging the agony for both parties.

Here are some examples of buried messages:

- ✗ So, Ray, how's your mother doing since your dad died? Is she still golfing? Oh, hey, by the way, we're unfortunately going to have to let you go - cutbacks from head office.
- ✗ Hey, Sarah – great to see you back. How was the cottage? You look like you got some sun! Hopefully you were using a good, strong sunscreen. Oh, the promotion? Right... well, we had to pass you over and give it to Jenny.
- ✗ You know, Kendra, we've so appreciated your work ethic and your sense of humor around here. In fact, even the cleaning lady comments on your smile and readiness to pitch in. You will be able to go anywhere with a personality like that – it's simply amazing. And, uh, speaking of "anywhere," did you hear that the company is outsourcing your entire department overseas?

In the examples above, the tension is palpable right away despite the fact that the bad news does not come until later on. If you have ever been a part of one of these conversations, you know that it doesn't matter whether you're on the giving end or the receiving end - they still feel awkward and terrible. By getting straight to the issue and choosing not to bury your message, you will ultimately just get the agony over with more quickly.

2. Give diplomacy a rest.

The diplomatic approach is all about trying to cushion the blow, so we foolishly censor our language to the point where no one could possibly understand what it is we are trying to say. If you have ever tried to talk to a bank that is turning down your loan request, then you know what I am talking about. Remember: hoping not to offend the other person is not a productive goal, even if it is a "nice" one. The reason we want to avoid tough conversations is largely because we are afraid of the other person's reaction - otherwise, it wouldn't be a very tough conversation, now, would it? But if you know it's going to be a difficult talk, then it's better to just say what you need to say and not censor yourself to the point of not being understood. When we avoid being clear for the sake of diplomacy, the integrity of the message suffers and we run the risk of either prolonging the pain in that conversation or being forced to have *multiple* conversations to get our point across - and nobody wants that.

Here's an example to mull over: what do you think the following might mean?

> "So, Marianne, the department has made a decision to revamp the organizational chart across the board. Positions will unfortunately be eliminated or moved but no one has to worry, there shouldn't be any job loss. This should be a fairly simple process."

Hmm. Definitely not a clear statement. Positions eliminated but no job loss? Do they think Marianne is stupid? This boss needs to get real and say what he really means.

Here is how the straight goods might sound. No diplomacy here, but a solid, clear message:

> "Marianne, I wanted to let you know the department is reorganizing and positions will be eliminated. We will do our best to limit job loss through attrition and we'll work together to find opportunities in other departments. This is unfortunately going to be a challenging time for everyone."

Much better and more honest!

But for those of you who are saying to themselves, "But the second message sounds terrible! Marianne is going to be more upset by that version!" well, you're probably right. Unfortunately, the reality is that downsizing is not happy news, so there is no point in trying to make it sound like happy news. Marianne may be upset by the second message, but she would be confused by the first - and it is always better to be upset but clear about what's going on than to be confused and hold false hope that maybe nothing bad will happen.

Remember, once all that waffling starts, it's easy to come across as insincere and meanwhile, your message gets lost in the shuffle. Even if your diplomacy is well intended, as soon as it compromises the clarity of your message, you have a serious problem on your hands.

3. Avoid the feedback sandwich.

You know how people tend to package bad or sad news between slices of good news or flattery? That's a feedback sandwich. Does the following feedback sandwich sound like good communication to you?

> "Well, your father did very well during surgery. Unfortunately, he coded in the recovery room and we lost him. The good news is that many of his organs are very healthy. Would you like to donate them to help out others?"

I didn't think so.

Now, it can be argued that there *is* a place for the feedback sandwich in some types of conversations, but these kinds of tough talks do not make the cut. Don't try to hide your news in far-reaching positives; all that will do is make you look like a jerk who does not appreciate how difficult the subject in question is for the other person.

4. Avoid blaming others.

Blaming others makes you look like a sellout or a tattletale and people always see through it immediately.

Consider this cringe-worthy example:

> "So, Gregory, I want you to know that I *really* put in a good word for you regarding the special project, but the director had already decided to give it to his nephew. I did what I could, but he pulled rank on me. If it had been up to me, the job would have been yours. Sorry, but you can't shoot the messenger, right?"

"Sure, that guy sounds like a dope," you might be saying, "but what if the situation at hand really *isn*'t my fault?" Even if the news isn't your fault, you won't gain anything by trying to make it sound as if someone else is to blame. Be the bigger person and don't lay the blame on somebody else. Instead, take ownership of your news.

5. Avoid the "wolf in sheep's clothing."

A "wolf in sheep's clothing" statement is when you say something that attempts to be diplomatic but comes across as an attack, criticism or judgment on the other person. Check this out:

> "Diane, I don't have an issue with changing plans. I just think we need to communicate *honestly* with each other about the reason for the change."

Hmm. Did you pick up on the implication that I am being dishonest about something? Somebody did actually say this to me once, so I can tell you firsthand that I felt slighted and defensive. Instead of accusing someone - indirectly or otherwise - remember to focus on the facts rather than your interpretation of the facts. Choose to be the straight shooter and say something like this:

> "Diane, you seem to be changing plans and I am wondering why."

Simple, direct and non-accusatory: a much stronger start to a productive conversation.

Your ABCs in Action: Ian the Interrupter

You now have the tools to create some excellent ABC messages. Let's take a look at a sample workplace conversation to see your toolkit in action.

Imagine you have a talkative coworker, Ian, who loves to interrupt you on a regular basis. It is really starting to bother you; you are feeling disrespected and you sense that your views don't matter (yup, that would be your inside voice talking!). Your self-respect is at stake as well as your relationship with Ian, so you decide you need to say something. Your goal is to let Ian know that you want to be heard and that you are frustrated with how discussions between the two of you often go. You want this to be a private conversation and you want to have it as soon as possible after the most recent "interruption incident," so the behavior is fresh in both of your minds. So, off you go to Ian's office with your prepared ABC message to talk to him about what happened at the team meeting today. What might you say?

> "Ian, *I am* not sure if you are aware that in our meeting today, you interrupted me while I was sharing my ideas on the Acme project. *I have experienced* you interrupting me on a number of occasions when we are having discussions. I *am feeling* really frustrated because *I* would like the opportunity to share my ideas fully." STOP TALKING. (Embracing silence empowers your message.)

This is a fabulous ABC message: accurate, brief and clear. Now Ian knows what is going on for you without any judgmental, subjective or "hot" language. You did not assume any negative intentions on his part. He is more likely to hear this message than if you had said that he "never listens" or "always interrupts," or if you had accused him of being rude or self-centered. This message is also much better because you chose to deliver it in private rather than getting sarcastic at the meeting and blurting, "Do you *mind* if I finish *one* sentence, Ian?" You successfully started this tough conversation by focusing on the correct goal, not assuming the worst and remembering your ABCs. Well done!

Top Tools to Recall: Designing Your ABC Message

- ✓ "A" is for "accurate:" stick to the facts and remember that your judgments and assumptions do not qualify as facts.
- ✓ "B" is for "brief:" aim for 30 seconds and definitely not more than 2 minutes.
- ✓ "C" is for "clear:" make your message direct and precise and avoid burying it in confusing language.
- ✓ Use "I" statements, such as "I think," "I am," "I believe," "I feel," etc.
- ✓ Avoid "hot," judgmental words such as "rude," "difficult," "lazy," "disrespectful," "disorganized," etc.
- ✓ Share the impact of the person's actions without blame, shame or judgment.

Great! Now you have created your message in a way that delivers the "straight goods" and, if all goes well, will still leave the other person feeling respected. As you can see, preparation is key because it helps you create the right frame of mind as well as find the words for a successful conversation.

Before delivering your message, however, it is essential to prepare yourself even further by anticipating the other person's potential reaction(s). Sure, *you* have had lots of time to think about this conversation and prepare for it, but the other person has not. Now it's time to get ready for how the other person responds to your news. If you don't, you risk being blindsided by all kinds of negative, scary and (dare I say) crazy reactions that, if handled improperly, will send your conversation into a tailspin. Preparation is essential so that you can keep your conversation on track.

Don't want to be caught like a deer in the headlights? Don't want your tough conversations to feel like sneak attacks that cause other people to fight with all of their might? You're about to find out how.

Tame the Elephant in the Office
(in 4 pretty easy steps)

Step 1: Prepare to Talk

Get clear about what the real issue is and write it down in three sentences or less. Then determine what your ultimate goal is for the conversation. Be realistic.

Step 2: Design and Deliver Your "ABC Message"

What do you say and how do you say it? It's as easy as "ABC:" make it Accurate, Brief and Clear. Don't waste your time dancing around the issue; be honest and give people the "straight goods" in a way that is respectful and nonjudgmental.

Step 3: Stop Talking and Start Listening

Once you have delivered your ABC message, listen without interruption to hear the other person out. This may be your toughest challenge, but it is essential to keep the conversation on track... and it is easier than you think!

Step 4: Respond Powerfully

This is your opportunity to respond (not react) and clarify in a way that is confident, concise and clear. No excuses. No justifications. No blame.

Chapter 7:

Delivering Your ABC Message

Chapter highlights:

- ☐ *Anticipate the other person's reaction to your message and mentally prepare yourself so you have the confidence that you can handle anything that comes your way.*
- ☐ *Set the stage for your conversation by asking permission and choosing the right time and place.*
- ☐ *Have the talk... because they deserve to know and you deserve to tell them.*

There are two final things you need to do before you launch yourself into your tough talk if you want to ensure your success: first, you need to anticipate how the other person might react to your ABC message so you can mentally ready yourself and, second, you need to set the stage for actually having the conversation. All of this groundwork will pay off when you finally deliver your message.

If we rush into a difficult conversation, we inevitably mess something up and, when we mess up, it takes a lot of additional time and energy to clean up the aftermath of all the confusion, hurt feelings, misunderstandings, etc. I have done my share of leaping in head first without thinking of the consequences, believe me; please, learn from my mistakes and choose to plan ahead! If you do, your conversations - and your work relationships - will reap the rewards.

Anticipate Their Reactions

In order to focus, stay on track and avoid rabbit holes, you need to anticipate and be ready for the inevitable reaction to your ABC message, no matter how brilliant it sounds in your head. Here's why: even the best ABC messages do not account for what the other person is going to say or do in response. Preparation by anticipating the other person's reactions gives you the best chance of success because all of your hard work won't be undermined by an unexpected response. You are well aware of your feelings about the conversation; after all, how many sleepless nights have you had over it? Now, it is time to consider how the other person might react to your message. Put yourself in his or her shoes: how would *you* react or feel and then ask yourself if the other person is likely to:

"Wisdom consists of the anticipation of consequences."
- Norman Cousins[16]

- ☐ Be hurt
- ☐ Get defensive
- ☐ Break into tears
- ☐ Threaten you
- ☐ Attack
- ☐ Beg
- ☐ Be embarrassed
- ☐ Make promises to change

Anticipating the other person's response and being prepared gives you the confidence to handle anything that might be thrown your way. It takes the sting out of the other person's reaction (if it actually happens) and helps you to remain neutral and detached. Remember, this is a tough talk that you have probably agonized over and potentially avoided out of fear of what could go wrong. If you visualize working out the worst-case scenario ahead of time, then you are ready and nothing could really faze you. Athletes use visualization in order to achieve peak performance, so why not use the same proven tactic in our own important conversations in order to be successful? A little prep work on your part in this arena will remove some of the anxiety that goes hand in hand with these conversations, which will ultimately help you to achieve your desired outcome.

Helpful Hint: Unhook Emotionally

Think about how you might get "hooked" in a conversation - something that could cause you to accidentally lose control. What is the other person likely to do or say that may cause you to react, rather than stay focused? Anticipate and plan for it. This will help you swim by the hooks and stay calm, cool and in control.

If you anticipate a reaction and the worst-case scenario doesn't materialize, then you'll be pleasantly surprised. Don't get me wrong here: I am not a pessimist, I am a realist. The goal here is to be able to stay collected and confident when in the hot seat. You want to be ready so that you can respond in a way that is aligned with your ultimate goal rather than react out of anger, fear or hurt feelings.

Story of Support

I want to share a story about how I prepared myself for a conversation to which I anticipated a defensive reaction. It was one of those situations where I was able to detach myself so that I did not react and the outcome was very positive. It was a reminder to me that this stuff really works if you stick with it.

"Expect the best. Prepare for the worst. Capitalize on what comes."

- Zig Ziglar

There was a time when I was making the transition from lawyer to consultant and was focused on education and learning. I was working from home and was more available and present for my family than I had been in the past. It was also a time when we did not have anyone helping out at home. Despite enjoying the learning part of my changing direction, I was starting to rot in my comfort zone, so I knew it was time to get things rolling. I secured my first speaking gig and designed my first workshop. I trained in difficult conversations and mediation at Harvard Law School. So now, of my own doing, I was out of my rut and flat out swamped with work.

The problem for me was the difficulty in managing it all: kids' activities, meals, the dog, work, travel and all that goes along with managing a house and a budding career. I felt that I wasn't at the stage where I could really justify hiring anyone as I was spending more money than I was earning (a familiar song for a lot of people). I was feeling downright resentful about all the "menial" work I was doing and I surpassed the dog when it came to barking at the kids and my hubby. "I am not the maid around here, you know!" I would screech. "Any one of you could help out at any point in time!" The mood around our house was deteriorating quickly. I decided I needed to have a productive conversation with my hubby about getting more support from him to manage it all. It was my sense (right or wrong) that I had previously asked for the help I needed and yet the help was not forthcoming. Obviously, we needed to talk before tensions got any worse.

I prepared for the conversation and I was pretty sure that this would be a touchy subject. Hubby sees himself as a supportive spouse (and he is) as well as a supporter of women in their careers. His mother was a successful career woman and he admires her and all she has accomplished. I broached the subject and told him from "my view" (which was my version of "the truth") that I was not getting the support from him that I needed. I was ready for a strong defensive reaction. After all, I know this man very well. The reaction came as I had anticipated and went something like this: "What do you mean? I think I am very supportive. I am more supportive than most men! I don't think you appreciate me and I don't think you are being fair."

I listened. I stayed present and remembered my goal was to get to some productive solutions on the subject of help for some of the mundane chores of life, not to get into a heated argument about whether he was a supportive husband. That argument would have served no purpose and would only have left both of us feeling miserable. Anticipating his reaction helped me to stay focused and not get "hooked." I chose to stay calm and be quiet despite the fact that I wanted to jump in, defend myself, bolster my position and possibly hurl a few unhelpful little digs.

The result? Within about 30 seconds (yes, it can be that fast), hubby calmly turned to me and said, "What do you need from me to get the kind of support you are looking for?" We then had a constructive conversation and worked out some solutions we were both happy with. If I had not taken the time to anticipate a defensive response (almost guaranteed in a situation like this) then I likely would have been embroiled in a long and drawn-out fight about unrelated and unimportant matters that I would later regret. To me it was a true sign that being prepared really works!

Setting the Stage

The final step in laying the groundwork for your conversation is to "set the stage." *You* are well prepared, but you do not want your conversation to feel like a sneak attack. Now you need to give the other person a heads-up that an important discussion is imminent. Here are a few strategies to assist you in preparing for a successful conversation:

1. Ask permission.

Asking permission to have a conversation works in both personal and business relationships. The act of asking permission to have a talk conveys respect. This strategy was working very well for me and I was doing it regularly until, one day, I wanted to talk to a close friend about a touchy subject: her intimate relationship.

When I asked her if I could talk to her about some concerns I had, she responded with an emphatic "no." Now what? This was someone I really cared about and I was worried about them. I tried to forge on and talk about my concerns anyway, which only caused an argument because she had expressly denied me permission to broach the subject.

The moral of the story is that if you ask for permission and the person says "no," then you need to respect that. Otherwise, you lose credibility and your request comes across as insincere (and, in fairness, it kind of would be). On the other hand, oftentimes in the workplace, having your difficult conversation is a must, for example when you need to talk to your assistant about some concerns with her work or to a coworker about missing deadlines. In those cases, you need to ask permission about the timing of the conversation, rather than asking permission to have the conversation at all. Ask if you can talk about your issues now and, if the other person says no, then you will have to be flexible and offer other options for a time to talk. Just be straightforward and say something like this:

> "I would like to set up a meeting sometime this week. Here are the options… What works best for you?"

2. *Choose the right time.*

Timing is crucial and immediacy is best. Generally, the sooner your conversation occurs after the incident in question, the better it is for everyone. Otherwise, the details get blurry and there is nothing like time to weave judgments and interpretations into a story. Your inside voice will try to use the time to get the upper hand, so try to have your talk sooner rather than later.

If, however, you are fuming about an incident and raring to blurt something out, then time is not the enemy. Button up until you are calm and thinking straight. Here is a useful rule of thumb from my son's hockey coach: take a 24-hour cooling-off period if emotions are running high. Resist the temptation to use the "bravery" your anger is giving you to lash out and always give yourself time and lots of deep breaths before you say anything so that you can approach the conversation from as neutral a perspective as possible.

On the other hand, you should avoid the temptation to leave the other person hanging indefinitely once you have requested a meeting. Don't make the other person wait a week while you juggle your yoga class, your coffee dates, your last-minute errands. Allowing too much lead time will cause both of you to fret and second-guess yourselves (and gives the other person plenty of time to gather their ammo!). It's not going to be pretty!

3. *Choose the right place.*

Location, location, location: it's critical in real estate and it's critical in your tough conversations. Think about the nature of your talk and your relationship with the other person when you are choosing the venue. In most cases, you don't want to have your difficult conversation in front of other people; a private discussion will help the other person avoid embarrassment or that awful feeling of being put on the spot, which will in turn reduce the likelihood of a big, ugly scene. It's just common sense: if you are firing someone, you don't do it "reality TV boardroom style;" behind closed doors in your office is much more sensitive and appropriate. Lunch in a busy restaurant could work if you are confessing to your best friend that, somehow, there is a cigarette burn on her favorite Donna Karan blazer that you borrowed last week, but not if you are having to tell your coworker that he needs to wear deodorant when you go into sales meetings. Remember to put yourself in the other person's shoes and ask yourself where *you* would want to hear the news that you are planning to share.

Amazing - you've done it! You are now ready to have this conversation that you have been *so* dreading. You have all of the tools you need; all that's left to do now is practice. Let's look at some workplace scenarios to see how you could craft and deliver a few great ABC messages:

Dealing With a Difficult Boss: Hounding Helen

It's coffee time at the office and you and a coworker have nipped out to get a quick latte and have a little office drama gripe session. The topic *du jour* is a work issue that you are reluctant to tackle. The long and short of it is that you feel that Helen, your boss, is micromanaging you like crazy. You have been having a lot of whining sessions lately and definitely not of the two-minute variety! Well, you have read my book, so you know that major complaining also means major avoiding. Now, it's time to take action.

After coffee, you begin creating your ABC message (accurate, brief and clear) for Helen. You are going to have to quiet your inside voice that has convinced you that it is true and factual that Helen is a micromanaging control freak, incessantly telling you what to do and when to do it. You need to take a mental dump here (always a good thing) and ask yourself what it is that Helen says or does that leads to you to say she micromanages you and why that is causing a problem.

The facts: Helen unfailingly asks you to meet with her twice a week to run all of your ideas by her. You feel demoralized and are concerned that she has doubts about your work and your ability. Your creativity and self-esteem are going down the toilet, not to mention that your coworker is sick and tired of all of your moaning. Your goal in having the conversation is to find out why Helen is making these requests and address her concerns. You also want to let her know how her micromanaging behavior is affecting you (although you are not going to use the word "micromanaging" because it implies criticism and judgment).

You anticipate this talk could be tough because Helen has a reputation for getting defensive. You know you do good work and you feel confident about what you contribute, so you feel ready to tackle this talk. You know that this is definitely a conversation you want to have in private and you need a cooling-down period after what you consider to be the latest in a long line of slights (darn that inside voice anyway!), so you ask for a meeting for the following day.

The next day, you deliver your ABC message with confidence:

"Helen, since you became my manager you have asked me to meet with you twice a week and to run all of my marketing ideas by you before I include them in the mock-up brochures. I'm not sure where you are coming from, but I am starting to wonder if you have concerns about my ability to do my job well. Can we talk about this?" STOP TALKING. (Hear her out and prepare to be surprised.)

This could be a fantastic start to a productive conversation about your work and Helen's management style. She is much more likely to hear this message than if you had said, "Helen, you are a control freak, always micromanaging me," or even worse, "Why can't you just trust my work? Everyone thinks you are a dyed-in-the-wool micromanager and you are driving us all crazy!" By now you know that statements like those never go over well. Stick with a calm and carefully designed ABC message to get your message heard!

Saying no: Spot-on Simon

You have just left a successful board meeting and are in the ladies' room putting on some lipstick and checking your phone when you see you have a new message from Spot-on Simon, one of your top producers. The message starts out casually enough, but then launches into how upset he is because he wasn't chosen to be part of the "Most Exciting Project Ever." You are surprised because you had already had this discussion with Simon several days ago. Now, he is suggesting he may leave the company if you refuse to add him to the new project team. You are taken aback by his subtle threats but manage to refrain from firing back a nasty email. Another manager walks into the ladies' room and you mention Simon's message to her and, to your surprise, she tells you that she'd already heard how upset Simon was because he has been telling anyone who would listen for days. Your inside voice is raging, "He is seriously unbelievable! I can't believe that Spot-on Simon, one of my key employees, is holding me hostage and telling everyone that he will quit if I don't put him on the project! Did he forget we just talked about this a few days ago? Where is his brain, anyway? He knows I can't run the department without him. After everything I've done for him, he stabs me in the back?"

Yes, it's time to talk to Simon with a clearly crafted ABC message. Remember, taking that mental dump really helps and don't forget to take a step back from the "hot," judgmental language of your inside voice. Facts are what will give you clarity on the problem. The facts are that Simon was not chosen to be a part of the big project and that you had advised him of this in a conversation that occurred several days ago. What is bothering you is that you have an over-confident employee testing you (with an audience no less). He is using a threat that cannot be tolerated because it would send the message that you can be manipulated. Your goal here is to let him know how much you value him and that you will not be reversing your decision. You anticipate that Simon is going to continue with his threats to leave but you are clear that you will not beg him to stay. So, if he tries more threats during your conversation, you feel confident that you can "swim by" that hook. He is not a part of this project, no matter how much you value him and hope that he won't actually make good on his threat to leave.

Now you are prepared to confidently deliver your ABC message:

> "Simon, we talked about this new project a few days ago and, as you know, I decided to put Mike on the project to get some experience. I know you disagree with my decision and you really want this gig. I understand that you are considering your options and may leave the organization if you don't get on this project. That is a choice that you will have to make. If you leave, it would be a huge loss for us. Having said that, please understand that I am not changing my decision. Ultimately you will have to decide where you go from here. If you decide to stay, then I expect that there will be no further discussion on this issue." STOP TALKING. (Remember that less is more.)

Spot-on Simon is much more likely to respect you if you talk to him this way than if you cave in, beg him to stay or make false promises for the future. Sure, he may be irritated or upset that his threatening to leave did not work, but had you caved or begged, you would essentially be telling Simon (and everyone else in your office) that he calls the shots and you don't - and news that the boss is a wuss always spreads like wildfire, so you would have been setting yourself up for a lot more problems down the road. This is a case where you absolutely needed to assert yourself by drawing a line in the sand.

Rude or Disrespectful Behavior: Dave and Darryl

Imagine you are the director of a non-profit organization. An hour ago, a lunch meeting was held with key participants from across the country. During the luncheon, two of the vital players, Dave and Darryl, began a private conversation, turning away from the group and excluding everyone else at the table. You were surprised and your inside voice started chattering right away, "Well, that's pretty rude! Now we all feel like we're getting picked last for the baseball team! How can these two be so unkind and unprofessional?"

Rather than wait, you decide to tackle the problem now and deliver a clear ABC message. First, you must nail down the issue and figure out your goal. In a nutshell, you are concerned about what impact this behavior will have on your working relationship with Dave and Darryl and how others at the lunch felt about being left out of their secret conversation. Your goal is simply to let them know your concerns. You anticipate that Dave and Darryl might be defensive, but you feel very strongly that they deserve to know. An opportunity to talk privately presents itself right away, so the stage is set.

Here is your ABC message:

"Dave and Darryl, I believe that you are great contributors to this field and, as experts, others are looking to you. I am concerned about the side conversation you just had at lunch and the message it sends to the rest of us that perhaps you have more important things to talk about. I'm not saying you shouldn't have confidential conversations, I just don't believe that the luncheon was the right time or place." STOP TALKING. (Let the message sink in.)

Surprisingly, Dave and Darryl are both appreciative of the heads-up and your willingness to be open with them about what had happened at lunch from your perspective. They were unaware of the impact of their behavior. You are pleasantly surprised, because you anticipated a defensive reaction and it didn't come - bonus! It was satisfying to realize that you will continue to have a good working relationship with Dave and Darryl rather than feel irritated and resentful had you not expressed your concerns. There was simply too much at stake to remain silent. Owning your opinions rather than presenting them as "the truth" was a key to successfully managing this tough talk.

However, imagine what would have happened with Dave and Darryl if instead you had said, "Your side conversation was so rude," or "You and Darryl were behaving so unprofessionally! What were you thinking?" This type of lead-in would have no doubt led to a defensive response and an awkward lunch to say the least.

Delivering Sensitive News: Ned the Nostril

You just landed an excellent job at a top-notch organization and you are so excited to join such an impressive team. The offices are fabulous, very modern and located in a high-energy downtown location. You know you have to be on your best behavior, especially in those see-through highly visible glass offices - certainly no quick changes in the office for a fast lunch-hour run! You and your coworkers have to be "on" all the time. It feels a bit like walking the red carpet at the Academy Awards - exciting, but also unforgiving.

One day, as you sat in your office, your gaze wandered over to your colleague Ned's office across the hall. Yuck! Ned was busy picking his nose with such vigor that you could not believe your eyes. Did he lose something up there? This was not one of those furtive, sneaky "oh, my nostril was just itchy" picks; he was digging for gold! You are completely shocked because this man is intelligent, well dressed and destined to be successful (or so you thought). What a social faux pas. Oh no, you think to yourself, I just really hope this was a one-time offense.

No such luck. You observe Ned time and time again picking his nose. One day, you see him with his finger up his nose while in a meeting with a client. You have talked to your coworkers and you all agree: someone has to say something and quick! There is so much at stake here: Ned's reputation, the reputation of the company, not to mention Ned's secretary, the poor girl who tidied up around his desk and took away his coffee cup. The visual is fairly horrifying. So, you draw straws for who is going to broach the subject and big surprise – you win (or lose)!

You start thinking about what you are going to say to Ned. The goal is just to let him know you have observed this behavior because you believe that he deserves to know (and sorry, offering him a box of tissue is not direct enough). The hard part is telling him about his habit. You anticipate that he will likely be embarrassed, but you respect this man and want to let him know what you have observed. One day you gingerly approach him in the confines of his office and ask him if you can talk to him about a sensitive issue. He agrees.

Then you say:

> "Ned, I am not sure if you are aware of it, but I have noticed you picking your nose on many occasions. At least once this happened when there was a client in your office. I didn't know how to broach this subject. I assumed you must be unaware that you were doing it and I thought you would want to know." STOP TALKING. (Brevity is better for all concerned here.)

As much as you might like to, there is no way to avoid embarrassment here. You anticipated the awkwardness, but this topic was just too important and you like Ned too much not to say anything. You don't try to soften the blow or ease his embarrassment (or yours); yet this kind of message is much more respectful than blurting out, "Stop picking your nose! It is disgusting!" or worse, not saying anything at all.

Delivering Bad News: Nightclub Natasha

You work with a smart and aspiring young professional woman named Natasha. You rely on Natasha's talent and expertise to put together awesome campaigns for clients. The problem? Well, she is dressing in a way that some might describe as "provocative:" low-cut blouses and short, tight skirts. Instead of looking like she is working in a professional office, she looks like she is heading to the nightclub after work. You have noticed it (it is hard to miss the cleavage or the lacy underwear) and clients have noticed it. Despite her talent, you are afraid to bring her onto new jobs because of what clients might think.

You care about Natasha and her future with the company because you genuinely believe she has a lot of talent. You want to support her success, which is why you believe that Natasha deserves to know how her apparel choices could potentially be affecting her blossoming career. To prepare, you carefully put together your ABC message and choose a private time and place to have this tough conversation with Natasha.

What could you possibly say?

> "Natasha, I want to talk to you about an awkward issue. I have noticed that many of your work outfits do not project the professional image we are looking for. Your work is top notch and I am concerned that your clothing choices may have a negative impact on your credibility with clients and the firm's willingness to let you work with clients. I thought you deserved to know." STOP TALKING. (Time is needed to let your message sink in.)

This is definitely an awkward conversation, yet Natasha may not know how her clothing choices could be influencing her credibility and ultimately her career. You have done a good job in not using judgmental or "hot" language in the delivery of your message, so she is more likely to be able to really hear what you have to say. Was it easy? Probably not... but remember that you are coming from the perspective of "Natasha deserves to know."

It reminds me of a time that one of the partners I worked with came up to me at large firm function to let me know that I had visible panty lines that could be seen through my beautiful red suit. I was horrified and grateful at the same time. I'd had no idea. If she had not told me, I may have continued to make the same mistake and it could have undermined my image. How humiliating! Can you imagine me doing battle in the courtroom with my underwear outlined for all to see? If that partner hadn't said anything to me, even today I might be standing up on stages delivering seminars on challenging conversations with panty lines showing! I shudder at the thought! Sure, that partner's words may have been embarrassing to hear, but far better to hear them than never to know.

Giving the Straight Goods: No Contract for You

Many times in my career as a consultant, I have submitted proposals to deliver workshops or presentations at events. I wish I could say I always get the gig but it just doesn't happen that way - at least not for me. More often than not, people are uncomfortable telling you that you didn't get the contract because they feel bad letting you down. In my experience, they will send you an email telling you that you had a great proposal but they have unfortunately chosen someone else, although they will be keeping your proposal on file for future reference. In some cases, people don't even respond and hope that you will just go away and never follow up with them. Avoiding the conversation is usually just their way of trying to soften the blow, but when you are on the receiving end of that avoidance, it can be extremely frustrating.

I did have a situation in which someone did a really great job communicating with me: I had made a personal connection with this person and she had indicated to me that I was going to be getting a contract for a speaking engagement with the organization she represented. However, her bosses had had a change of heart and decided to go with another provider. I knew she felt bad because she had led me to believe that the contract was mine. Her goal in talking to me was to be honest with me that there was no contract and to do it in a way that was respectful and clear. She gave me the courtesy of a phone call and said something like this:

> "Diane, I don't know how to say this: The leadership team has decided on a different contractor. I was surprised and disappointed by the decision and I apologize for telling you that you had the deal."

As you can see, there was no long song and dance about "oh, your proposal is fabulous" or "we so look forward to working with you in the future." Comments like those would have just come across as insincere. After the conversation, she asked me how she had done with her tough talk. In my opinion, she had done an excellent job of delivering difficult news in a way that left me feeling respected. I gave her the thumbs up on a job very well done.

A Final Thought

Congratulations! You have successfully delivered your ABC message. You did a lot of preparation, which is exactly what is necessary to pull off a difficult conversation successfully. While you may feel scared or anxious when you don't know exactly what the outcome will be, if you prepare, anticipate and practice having these conversations you will gain confidence. I recommend you start with conversations where the stakes are lower to hone your skills and increase your confidence. As these talks become more natural to you (and trust me, they will), then you will be ready to face your most challenging conversations in the workplace.

Top Tools to Recall: Delivering Your ABC Message

- ✔ Be prepared by anticipating the other person's potential reactions. Knowing what may be coming will help you stay calm, cool and confident.
- ✔ Prepare the other person for your message by setting the stage: ask permission, choose the right time (the sooner, the better) and choose the right venue.
- ✔ Deliver your message while remembering your ABCs: be accurate, brief and clear.

Right now is the moment when many people are tempted to stop. You have finally delivered your message and, really, shouldn't that be it? You did a good job and you just want the stress and worry to be behind you - but I am afraid that your difficult conversation isn't over quite yet.

Now is the time to stop talking and start listening to the other person and find out what he or she heard in your message and what his or her perspective is on the matter. Let's face it: if you both agreed on the subject at hand, you probably would not have needed to have a conversation in the first place. Luckily, I do have some tricks up my sleeve for you to borrow if you want to have your tough talk go as smoothly as possible. The next part of your difficult conversation begins with listening.

Tame the Elephant in the Office

(in 4 pretty easy steps)

Step 1: Prepare to Talk

Get clear about what the real issue is and write it down in three sentences or less. Then determine what your ultimate goal is for the conversation. Be realistic.

Step 2: Design and Deliver Your "ABC Message"

What do you say and how do you say it? It's as easy as "ABC:" make it Accurate, Brief and Clear. Don't waste your time dancing around the issue; be honest and give people the "straight goods" in a way that is respectful and nonjudgmental.

Step 3: Stop Talking and Start Listening

Once you have delivered your ABC message, listen without interruption to hear the other person out. This may be your toughest challenge, but it is essential to keep the conversation on track... and it is easier than you think!

Step 4: Respond Powerfully

This is your opportunity to respond (not react) and clarify in a way that is confident, concise and clear. No excuses. No justifications. No blame.

Step 3:

Stop Talking and Start Listening

- Chapter 8: It's a Talk, not a Lecture
- Chapter 9: Dealing With Defenses
- Chapter 10: Managing Freak-Outs
- Chapter 11: Tools to Stay Cool
- Chapter 12: Tell Me More

Chapter 8:

It's a Talk, not a Lecture

Chapter highlights:

- ☐ *Listen to understand and acknowledge the other person's perspective, concerns and feelings.*
- ☐ *Listen by turning the conversation over, embracing silence, being curious, asking open-ended questions and calming your inside voice.*
- ☐ *Clarify if needed.*

"Courage is what it takes to stand up and speak; courage is also what it takes to sit down and listen."

- Sir Winston Churchill

Now that you have finally delivered your ABC message, you probably feel some relief and now you just want it all to be over. You aren't out of the woods yet, however; the moments following the delivery of your message are often the most important as well as the most difficult. Once the other person fixes you with that blank stare, incredulous look or dropped jaw, the temptation is very strong to babble on and on and on. Resist the urge. The other person simply needs time to process your message and respond. Allowing space to let the message sink in is not only powerful, but it is also definitely to your advantage. I can tell you that if you keep chatting the other person up, it will inevitably water down your message, diluting its impact and quite possibly resulting in you compromising or backing down before the other person has ever said a word in response. At this stage, we risk sabotaging ourselves *and* our message by not knowing when enough is enough. The best chance for a positive outcome with your difficult conversation is to stop talking as soon as your ABC message has been delivered - then start listening.

I Already Know How to Listen, Don't I?

The Merriam Webster Online Dictionary defines listening as: "to hear something with thoughtful attention: give consideration."[17] Yes, it sounds simple in theory, but putting it into practice is something else entirely, especially in the context of a difficult conversation. You might secretly harbor the hope that the other person will come around to your way of thinking without having anything to say about your ABC message, but chances are good that at least some listening on your part will be required in order to keep things on track.

There are two important reasons for listening:

1. You want to find out exactly what the other person has heard out of your ABC message. Brace yourself: you might be surprised by what you learn. The bottom line is that a message sent is not necessarily the message received, despite your meticulous preparation and good intentions.

2. You want to find out where the other person is coming from. What is the story from his or her perspective? People will always have their own points of view on the issues you raise and they are going to want you to hear them out. Keep in mind that people are much more likely to hear and accept your messages if they believe you have really heard and understood their perspectives and concerns first. This is a personal motivator for me and I am constantly reminding myself, "Diane, listen to them first and they are way more likely to take in your message." Maybe this sounds a little self-serving, but it works!

Okay, so the goal of listening is to understand what other people have heard *and* to be clear about their perspectives, concerns and feelings. By listening, you help the other person to feel heard, which in turn makes your message that much easier to digest.

The First Step in Listening: Shut Up

I used to think that listening simply meant not talking. I now know that, although there is more to it than that, not talking is a fabulous start. In theory, we know we have to stop talking in order to listen, yet in practice, it is often another story.

I have a talkative and friendly colleague, "Loquacious Larry," whom I run into from time to time. Larry loves to talk even more than I do; if you can escape a conversation with him in less than an hour, you are doing well. One day, he and I got into a discussion about what I was up to and I told him about the mediation course I took at Harvard Law School. He was so excited that he jumped in to tell me all about his experience with mediation. He even shared the most important lesson he had learned: "You know, Diane what I have learned is that if you are talking you can't learn anything. It has been a great reminder for me to listen." Ironic, huh? Well, believe me, that wasn't the end. He then proceeded to blab on and on for another 30 minutes, barely coming up for air! The lesson is that the "stop talking" message is great in theory, but practicing it can really be difficult.

The Good News: Listening Can Be Learned

Okay, maybe Loquacious Larry still has a way to go, but listening is a skill that *can* be learned with practice and, more importantly, a real commitment. It is like going on an exercise program: if you are patient and you stick with it, you will be ecstatic with the results. You will need a little willpower (or maybe a lot, depending on how much you love to talk) and a willingness to do things differently. Knowing that listening is the right thing and the efficient thing to do in your tough conversations should provide the incentive needed to sharpen your listening skills.

For me, understanding the power of listening was a real motivator - and if *I* can learn to really listen, believe me, anyone can (maybe even Loquacious Larry!). I come from a long line of incessant talkers; everyone in my family loves to hear the sound of their own voices and - I'm a little embarrassed to say - tends to prefer that sound over all others.

Let me paint the picture for you:

There are few family dinners in the Ross household where you are able to finish a sentence, let alone a whole thought, without people interrupting and weighing in with their own viewpoints. Family members often have input into multiple conversations going on at the same time and take pride in that (kind of bizarre) skill. If you can't get anyone to listen, you put up your hand to signal that you are next in line to speak your mind. Believe me, I know it sounds crazy; sometimes our dinner table looks more like a class in session than a family meal. I was one of the worst offenders - not a shocker I suppose - and it is only with the greatest discipline and resolve that I was ever able to keep my mouth shut long enough for someone else to finish a sentence. Ours is a household where dinner guests are shell-shocked after their first meal with the family. The din is absolutely deafening and many an intelligent and talkative newcomer was effectively silenced by the chaotic dynamics of a typical Ross family dinner.

I will never forget giving my hubby a hard time for not participating in our family gabfests early on in our relationship. "My family thinks you don't like them because you never say anything at dinner," I would complain. "You just sit there. Why can't you just say *something*? Anything would be good!"

His exasperated response to me was something like, "Diane, it is hard to imagine saying anything when everyone is talking at the same time over each other and never coming up for air. It gets louder and louder by the minute! I couldn't get a word in even if I'd wanted to." Well, as hard as it might be to believe, my hubby's words were news to me. My extremely talkative behavior was (and is) so ingrained in my psyche that even today listening requires ongoing effort and vigilance on my part.

Yes, real listening is difficult, but not hopeless. Here is the proof:

Not that long ago, hubby was talking to me about an issue that had come up at work. I was really focusing and practicing my newfound listening skills. I nodded my head and tried to really take in what he was saying. I even tossed in a few "umms" and "I sees" to show that I was staying present and interested in what he was saying. After a minute or so, he looked at me and said, "Are you okay? Is everything all right with you?"

I replied, "Of course! Why do you ask?"

He said, "Well you aren't saying anything. You aren't talking."

I responded, "I am listening to you, and I can't talk and listen at the same time."

He was a bit surprised - okay, maybe even floored - and then he said, "Wow, that is really awesome." Music to my ears!

Tools to Become a Better Listener

Here are a few tools I have used to improve my own listening skills (beyond just shutting my mouth, I mean):

1. Turn the conversation over.

After you have delivered your ABC message, be mindful about turning the conversation over to the other person. Just stop talking and take a brief pause; that's all that is necessary to give the other person tacit permission to jump in. Then all you usually have to do is simply embrace silence and listen. Easy as pie!

Of course, no talk is going to be entirely predictable and at other times you may have to work a little harder to turn the conversation over. Here are some questions and comments that will help nudge the other person to start contributing:

- ✔ Tell me what is going on from your perspective.
- ✔ What do you think about what I just said?
- ✔ What is your understanding of what I have said?
- ✔ What is your take on this?
- ✔ How do you see things?
- ✔ Tell me what is going on for you right now.
- ✔ I'm curious about your perspective on this.

The key here is to choose questions or statements that feel natural to you and then add them to your own personal list of techniques for turning your difficult conversations over to the other person.

2. *Embrace silence.*

Your questions have turned the conversation over to the other person and now you need to embrace silence. As one of my professors so eloquently said, it is important to "shut the duck up." The other person needs uninterrupted time in order to really respond to you and, once you have given that time, you both stand a better chance of reaching a resolution that really works. Be comfortable with silence and resist the temptation to fill it up with empty chatter. Many of us, myself included, are terrified of silence; just ask a lawyer, your best friend or a talk show host. Why do we chatter on? It could be because we want to help the other person and/or avoid the discomfort of silence. Yes, silence can be uncomfortable, but embracing silence is powerful because it signals confidence and removes the drive to compete for a turn to talk. I like to remind myself to marinate in the silence. Just like a steak, the end product is invariably much better when you do!

3. *Listen with curiosity.*

The conversation has been turned over and now the other person is telling you his or her side of the story. Now is the time to pay close attention to what is said and possibly to what is left unsaid. Simply holding your tongue is not enough; you have to actually focus. What did the other person hear you say? What are his or her concerns? What is his or her perspective? What really matters to the other person? You might think you already know all of this stuff since you did your best to anticipate the other person's reactions in the last chapter, but here is the thing: if the story were the same for both of you, you probably wouldn't need to be having this conversation in the first place... so pay attention.

Work hard to put yourself in the other person's shoes and always remember that you are listening with purpose, which translates to meaningful listening and is therefore very powerful. Do not gaze off into space. Do not casually check your smartphone. Do not cut the other person off mid-sentence. This kind of behavior will not go unnoticed and could cause your conversation to degenerate from "tough" to "total nightmare."

I think back to when I first read stories to my children; they *listened* to the story and then asked questions about the good guy, the bad guy, the best friend, etc. Then they *listened* to my answers.

They didn't have any preconceived notions, assumptions or ideas about how the story would end or even how or why the characters behaved as they did. That is the kind of listening I am talking about: learn to listen with curiosity and an open mind, just like children do (before they learn to talk back, anyway).

"Wisdom is the reward you get for a lifetime of listening when you'd rather have been talking."

- Aristotle

Even if you think you know "the truth," be open and receptive to another story. No matter how convinced you are that your assumptions are correct, you may be surprised to learn something new. We have all experienced a time when we stormed angrily into a conversation only to discover that our upset feelings were based on a misunderstanding (e.g. "What do you mean you didn't steal my lucky pen? Oh, uh, it's right here in my drawer. Er, sorry"). What a waste of energy! Instead of clinging to your own preconceived notions, listen intently and ask questions only when the other person has finished talking - no interrupting. You might be amazed by what you can learn!

4. *Calm your inside voice.*

One of the secrets to listening attentively is being able to quiet your inside voice in real time. We talked about this a little in chapter three, so you know you need to hush your inside voice before you can craft a solid ABC message, but what about when your inside voice is *still* chattering away once your difficult conversation has started? We have all been guilty at some point of listening more to the snappy retorts of our inside voices than to what the other person is actually saying. We present a facade of listening (some better than others), but we are too busy formulating our counterargument to be able to hear what is actually going on. We want to be ready to pounce the minute the other person slows down to take a breath. This is listening to respond, not true listening. We may have heard the words, sort of, but we haven't really listened and therefore don't understand the other person's story at all.

The kind of listening we want to practice is listening with curiosity in order to genuinely understand the other person's perspective. Now is the time to calm your inside voice because you simply cannot listen while your inside voice is blabbering on and on. Remember, to calm your inside voice, it is very helpful to do a "mental dump," which means letting go of your beliefs, assumptions and judgments. Then, ask yourself *why* the other person would say what they are saying. What are the main concerns here and how does this situation look from his or her perspective? Everyone wants to be heard and understood, so if you're aiming for a successful conversation (and I sure hope you are!), you need to calm your inside voice and really *hear* the other person. Yes, it can be tough, but if you commit to improving your ability to listen by being curious and quelling your inside voice, I promise you will be pleasantly surprised by the results.

Ask Good Questions

Awesome! You've listened to the other person. Now what? Well, now you are ready to ask some "tell me more" questions that do not presume to already know the answer. Asking a "tell me more" question will get you the answers you need to dig deeper into an issue. The goal is to gain a thorough understanding of the other person's perspective so you can move forward in your conversation.

Here is an example of what I'm talking about:

Your boss says you are not getting the promotion you were hoping for because you have not shown initiative. You assume that "initiative" means working long hours and taking on lots of projects and assignments, all of which you have done. You leave the meeting fuming and can't stop stewing over it, so you decide you need to talk to your boss. When you do finally meet with him, you tell him that you are upset that you did not get the promotion because you believe that you have shown lots of initiative. He flat-out disagrees and you are left even more frustrated than before you walked in to that conversation.

The problem: you never asked your boss what he meant by "initiative." What does it mean to him? His version of initiative may be very different than yours (in fact, at this point you can probably count on it). Maybe your boss perceives initiative as taking the lead on projects and making tough decisions, which is something you have shied away from. Maybe he means picking up weekend shifts, which you haven't done because you prefer to reserve weekends for family time. "Initiative" could mean any number of things here, so you are going to have to take the bull by the horns and find out exactly what your boss was looking for so you *will* get the promotion you're after sooner rather than later. Your "tell me more" question might be:

> "Would you tell me more about what 'initiative' looks like to you?"

Then, as your boss explains his definition of "initiative," your job is to listen to *understand*, not to argue or disagree. Sure, maybe you are still upset and have some choice words brewing for your boss, but letting your inside voice get involved is not going to help, especially if you are serious about getting that promotion.

Here are some more examples of "tell me more" questions:

- ✔ I never thought of it about that way. Tell me more about your perspective.
- ✔ I don't understand. Would you please tell me more?
- ✔ How do you feel about this? Tell me more.
- ✔ I am wondering what information you have relied on to reach that conclusion; tell me more.
- ✔ Tell me more about why this is important to you.
- ✔ You seem concerned; please tell me more.

The questions above help you to learn more about the other person's side of the story so that you both can be as clear as possible. On the flip side, it can be pretty easy to dress up your assumptions and judgments as questions (usually your inside voice is the culprit), but these are not true "tell me more" questions and will not propel your conversations in the right direction. Take a look at some of these "questions:"

- ✗ Do you really think it's okay to arrive late to our meetings?
- ✗ You aren't really going to leave before the reports are done, are you?
- ✗ Don't you think if you had put more effort in, we might have landed the contract?
- ✗ You know you weren't being very responsible here, right?

If you have ever been asked something like this, you know how terrible it feels and how quickly you can get your back up. These types of "questions" are closer to a courtroom cross-examination than a "tell me more" question and will certainly put the other person on the defensive. Don't go there, no matter how tempting. Keep your focus on embracing silence, asking good questions and really listening to the other person's answers instead of your inside voice chatter. This is how you create good listening habits.

Acknowledge the Other Person

Acknowledgement lets the other person know that you paid attention, that you listened. I used to think that if I acknowledged other people's views or perspectives, it implied either that I agreed with them or that they were right and I was wrong (not my favorite thing). Not so. I discovered through my research that acknowledgement is not about agreement or backing down. It is actually another very powerful way of showing that I am paying attention and that I am trying to understand what is going on for the other person. Once I realized that acknowledgment conveyed strength, not weakness, I was able to practice acknowledgement much more freely in my difficult conversations.

Ultimately, acknowledgment is about creating an atmosphere of respect, even in your toughest of conversations. Here are two ways for you to acknowledge the other person's story:

1. *Summarize in your own words what your understanding is of the other person's perspective and concerns.*

Use keywords and language that is consistent with who you are as a person. Do not parrot, mimic or otherwise repeat what the other person said to you because it sounds contrived and does not show that you actually heard the other person. My son likes to remind me that parroting works for birds, not for people.

To acknowledge other person's point of view, try these phrases:

- ✔ Let me make sure I understand what you're saying...
- ✔ All right, what I think you are saying is...
- ✔ It seems to me that you are saying...
- ✔ The way I hear it is...
- ✔ It sounds like you think that...

Again, you will want to try these kinds of phrases on for size and see what feels genuine and authentic to you. The idea here is not to have an arsenal of canned responses but rather a toolkit full of resources to help you convey your genuine acknowledgement of what the other person is saying.

2. *Acknowledge their feelings.*

Acknowledging someone else's feelings is about letting the other person know you are making a sincere effort to "get it." It is about putting yourself in someone else's shoes, which demonstrates empathy. This can be done with words, a nod of the head or simply staying physically present and connected to the conversation. Remember how my hubby was stunned that I actually listened to his work issue? The difference in *how* I listened - by staying present, interjecting little "hmms" and "I sees" and not interrupting - made an immediate and palpable difference to him. The person you are having the conversation with will notice and appreciate your efforts, too.

Watch that you do not confuse empathy with sympathy. Sympathy is simply feeling compassion (i.e. feeling sorry) for someone, as in: "Oh, that is just too horrible," "I would just die if someone said that," or "Oh no, I went through the same thing when..." But too much sympathy can feel fake and can make the other person mutter things like: "Hey, this is *my* issue, not yours - get over yourself!" or "Don't pretend to care how I feel right now!" If you say to someone, "I understand how you feel," despite your good intentions their knee-jerk response is invariably, "No, you do *not* know how I feel," or "Don't act like you care about this as much as I do!" Sympathy can shut down communication. Empathy, on the other hand, respects people's independence and shows that you care about their feelings without making assumptions about *how* they're feeling.

Try some of these phrases to acknowledge the other person's feelings or concerns with empathy:

- ✔ It seems to me...
- ✔ I hear you saying...
- ✔ You seem upset/hurt/disappointed etc.
- ✔ I notice that...
- ✔ I can understand why you would be upset/hurt etc.

In summary, acknowledging other people shows them that you are listening and attempting to understand their perspectives, concerns and feelings. Remember, acknowledgement is not agreement or a "you win, I lose" scenario, so you can be genuine in your acknowledgment without fear that you are weakening your message. Being authentic as you acknowledge is key; if you come across as mechanical and insincere, you will not create an atmosphere of respect and the other person may feel patronized and then get defensive. Remember to choose words that feel natural. For practice, test your acknowledgment skills out on loved ones to see what works and feels right for you. My entire extended family has served as guinea pigs for my research, so why not enlist yours to help you out, too?

Clarify If Needed

As you are listening to the other person, you might hear things that just don't make sense and you may begin to wonder if your intended message was actually understood. If so, it is definitely okay to clarify what the other person's understanding of your message is. You may simply need to clear something up or dig a little deeper. That's perfectly normal - this is a dialogue, after all, with two people exchanging their perspectives and opinions. Never shy away from clarifying when necessary or you risk having to start your conversation all over again from scratch another day.

If and when you do find yourself needing to clarify, always choose your words and tone carefully so you do not come across as condescending. You may feel like a broken record, but if you speak as though you are frustrated for having to repeat yourself or as if the other person is stupid for not understanding you the first time around, you are setting your conversation up for a major downturn. If the other person did not understand you on the first try, reword your point (versus using the same exact language) and make sure to keep your tone neutral, not irritated or impatient. Remember that you are trying to keep an environment of respect, not of criticism or judgment.

Taking the Time: Mother Knows Best

By now, you might be saying, "Are you kidding? I don't have time for all of this!" I admit that it does sound like a lot - but "a lot" doesn't always mean it takes a lot of time, especially not once you have mastered the basics of managing tricky conversations. Listening and acknowledging does not mean you have to have a long, drawn-out conversation. In fact, when people feel heard, they often don't feel the need to repeat themselves over and over again, so ultimately your challenging talks get shorter.

I have experimented with taking the time to listen and it really does work to keep things concise. I did this once with my mother who, like a lot of mothers, loves to give me endless advice. I decided that the next time it happened, I would listen and acknowledge her point of view rather than get into a lengthy, irritating debate. Here is how it went down:

I went to visit my mom just before I was about to do a workshop. The elevator was out of service in her building and she was concerned about me lifting my heavy rolling briefcase down the stairs and out to my vehicle. So, she told me her plan for how "we" should get the briefcase down the stairs and to the car. Now, you have to understand that my mother had just had a hip replacement and wasn't going anywhere - certainly not down the several flights of stairs with me and my suitcase!

Normally, in these kinds of situations, I would grumble things like, "I think I'm old enough to figure out how to get my briefcase to the car" and "Why doesn't she just mind her own business?" My irritation with my mom would be reflected in my body language, my tone of voice and my facial expressions. We would then have a bit of a debate about the issue. I would stand my ground and she would accuse me of not listening to her.

On the day in question, I calmed my inside voice and said to myself, Why is mom telling me this? It's because she is trying to be helpful and is worried about me carrying my large briefcase. With that in mind, I was able to have a mental dump and actually listen to her grand plan. I then acknowledged her by saying something like, "It sounds like you are concerned about me carrying my briefcase and you think it would be a good idea to bring my car to the loading zone."

Mom replied with a simple "yes," but she was definitely a little shocked because, based on a lot of past experience, she had expected me to push back and be argumentative. She was refreshingly satisfied that I had listened to her point of view and I was delighted to realize that acknowledging her perspective did not mean I had to accept or follow her advice. It was really about respecting my mom and her views - and I got to avoid an argument with a person I love (and still carry on as planned).

If you are still unsure about acknowledging another person's perspective, feel free to try it out on a close family member, as I did. Then expect to be very pleased when you realize how easy it can be to circumvent an argument and shorten a tough talk simply by conveying respect through acknowledgment.

Uncovering the Bigger Picture: Tardy Tina

Let's look at a common work dilemma: the late employee or coworker. It's easy for your inside voice to get carried away in a heartbeat here, but sometimes there is more to the story than first meets the eye. You may be surprised by what you can learn and the creative solutions you can uncover simply by listening.

Let's say that one of your key staff members, Tardy Tina, consistently arrives late for work. As luck would have it, Tardy Tina is one awesome employee and you've been lax in taking any action against her perpetual lateness because you don't want risk losing her. Unfortunately, now other employees are complaining that Tina is getting special treatment; you realize that you can't stall any longer without risking your reputation as a leader. It's time to take some direct action.

So, what are the real facts? Tardy Tina has been late 16 times in the past month. You have made an assumption that Tina thinks she is above the rules because of her otherwise awesome work ethic, but you know that assumptions do not equal facts and therefore may have no bearing on the real story. Although you are irritated, you remind yourself to quell your inside voice so that you and Tina can have a genuine dialogue to get to the root of the issue.

You initiate your talk, letting Tardy Tina know how many times she has been late this month; then you stop talking so that your message can sink in. As you had anticipated, Tina defends herself, reminding you she commutes further than most, is a consistently high producer and stays late whenever needed. You are tempted to react to her excuses, but you resist. Instead, you simply listen and then acknowledge that everything Tina said is true. A clarifying question would now serve well, something like: "I wonder if you would tell me why you've been late so many times *this* month. Is there something going on that I should know about?" Initially, there is silence, but then Tina unloads and, as you get the real truth, your assumptions fly out the window.

It turns out that Tina drops her young daughter off at the school bus stop every morning on her way to work, but on dark, cold, wet winter mornings has a hard time leaving her standing there alone. You completely understand her dilemma, so you ask, "Do you have any ideas how we could resolve this?" Tardy Tina suggests flexing her hours to start 15 minutes later in the morning and stay 15 minutes later in the afternoon. As she had already pointed out, she often stays late in the afternoon anyway, so this is a good solution for her and you now have someone you can count to be there each day to close up shop. You agree and later notify the rest of the staff that Tardy Tina's hours have changed. You clarify with Tina your expectations that, with her new work hours, she will be on time for work each day.

Good job! By letting go of your assumptions, opening up an honest dialogue with Tina and then really being present for what she had to say, you were able to come up with a creative solution. Not only do Tina's new hours benefit the both of you, but the rest of your staff now knows that you are a fair employer who is willing to work with them to find appropriate solutions to real-life problems. This is just one scenario, but the principle applies to virtually endless workplace situations: by listening, you can learn a lot and avoid getting unnecessarily worked up about assumptions and judgments that never needed to be made. When you listen and keep an open mind, you pave the way to a productive conversation and a better overall outcome.

Summing Up

Remember that to use the tools and skills here, you must be genuinely interested in what the other person is saying and feeling. If you are not interested, it will shine through in your body language: I am talking about zoning out, blank stares, crossed arms, tapping toes, smartphone checks, etc. Do not assume the other person won't mind your more-than-obvious signals. Instead, commit to engaging and giving the other person the gift of your attention. Don't worry about responding for now; you will get your opportunity later on, so just sit back, relax and pay attention to what the other person is saying *right now*. When you listen and acknowledge, you take the competition out of your talk and the other person will feel heard, which will make it more likely that you will also be listened to. The end result is that your tough conversation will be over faster and likely with much more desirable results.

Top Tools to Recall: Listen Instead of Lecture

- ✔ Once you have delivered your message, turn the conversation over to the other person so he or she has the opportunity to respond.
- ✔ Show confidence by embracing silence.
- ✔ Learn to stifle your inside voice in real time.
- ✔ Ask good questions, listen to understand, and acknowledge the other person's perspectives, concerns and feelings.

Wow! First, you prepared and delivered your ABC message. Then, you embraced silence and turned the conversation over to the other person. You stopped talking and asked good "tell me more" questions to really get to the heart of the issue. You listened intently and with curiosity. Next, you acknowledged the other person's perspective, concerns and feelings. Whew! Congrats on a job well done!

Now, here is the catch: this process so far assumes that everything has gone pretty smoothly in your difficult conversation. However, the reality is that no matter how prepared you are or how perfect your ABC message is, things can go sideways in the blink of an eye. Human beings are complicated and we never quite know for sure how people will respond to our messages, even when we do our best to anticipate. If the other person doesn't "see the light" right away, how are you going to manage the response to keep the conversation on track? Don't worry: I'm not going to throw you to the wolves now when you have already come so far! There *are* ways to deal with defensive or otherwise unwelcome reactions in your tough conversations, so let's take a look at those next.

Tame the Elephant in the Office
(in 4 pretty easy steps)

Step 1: Prepare to Talk

Get clear about what the real issue is and write it down in three sentences or less. Then determine what your ultimate goal is for the conversation. Be realistic.

Step 2: Design and Deliver Your "ABC Message"

What do you say and how do you say it? It's as easy as "ABC:" make it Accurate, Brief and Clear. Don't waste your time dancing around the issue; be honest and give people the "straight goods" in a way that is respectful and nonjudgmental.

Step 3: Stop Talking and Start Listening

Once you have delivered your ABC message, listen without interruption to hear the other person out. This may be your toughest challenge, but it is essential to keep the conversation on track... and it is easier than you think!

Step 4: Respond Powerfully

This is your opportunity to respond (not react) and clarify in a way that is confident, concise and clear. No excuses. No justifications. No blame.

Chapter 9:

Dealing With Defenses

Chapter highlights:

- ☐ *"Shut the duck up."*
- ☐ *Avoid responding to the other person's defensiveness.*
- ☐ *Help the other person save face.*

When you have worked so hard to craft and deliver a productive ABC message, then are intent on really listening to the other person, it can seem supremely unfair when you are met with an upset, hostile, unkind or otherwise defensive reaction. It is definitely challenging to listen and keep the talk on track when people respond defensively in your difficult conversations and, although you might wish and hope and pray that they won't get defensive, chances are high that they will - so it's best to be prepared.

What exactly do I mean by a defensive response? If they start making excuses or denying that they said or did something, that is a defensive response. If they start in with the blame game or drone on and on with lengthy explanations, that is a defensive response. Although defensiveness can complicate your difficult conversations, it is a completely natural knee-jerk reaction when someone feels embarrassed, disappointed or criticized. Hey, this is a tough talk, right? Dealing with someone's defenses is just part of the deal. If you learn how to manage these responses, you are setting yourself up for success in your difficult conversations.

Now that the other person's defenses have kicked in, your discussion is no longer an intellectual exercise; this is where the rubber meets the road. The good news: your response to the other person's defensiveness will guide where things go from here. You influence big time the other person's reactions to your message throughout the conversation.

"Circumstances are beyond human control, but our conduct is in our own power."

- Benjamin Disraeli[18]

If you react negatively to the other person's defensiveness, it adds fuel to the fire. Even if he or she is acting like a complete twit, jumping in to interrupt, correct or counter what is being said is like dumping a whole bunch of gasoline-soaked newspapers on your fire and then lighting them with a blowtorch. Resist the urge to react or you might end up burning down the whole office.

Remember that your goal is to have a successful conversation about an issue or concern that is important to you, not to get involved in a long-winded discussion about unrelated or less important issues. Reacting to the other person's defensiveness is a surefire way to sidetrack the conversation. So what are you supposed to do if not defend yourself in kind? The key is to pay attention to the other person and let the defensiveness fizzle out naturally. One way to do that is to remind yourself to "shut the duck up" - if you aren't talking, then you aren't reacting!

What Is Defensiveness Really About?

Defensiveness is a primal instinct. Often, people feel compelled to respond defensively over even the most innocent of comments. Quite recently, I was invited to a potluck dinner party and I was put on salad duty. We were in the kitchen enjoying a glass or two of Chardonnay and a gab session (both of which I happen to love). With dinner almost ready, I started to prepare my salad and was just about to pour on the dressing when my girlfriend said to me, "Diane, don't toss the salad yet."

I immediately shot back, "Hey, I know! I wasn't going to!" even though I had the lid off, clearly poised to pour my (if I do say so myself) fabulous salad dressing. We laughed about it later, but why on earth did I automatically respond so defensively? We are talking about a salad here!

Dictionary.com defines defensiveness as: "excessively concerned with guarding against the real or imagined threat of criticism, injury to one's ego or exposure of one's shortcomings."[19] Even if we do not intend to come across as critical, our message might be perceived that way. If you say to your colleague, "You were late for the client lunch today. What's up?" she may react by saying, "Well, I am not the only one who is ever late. You are late sometimes, too! Who are you to criticize me? I work hard!" Responses like this leave us reeling because we can't figure out what it was we said that set them off. Usually, the culprit is criticism, whether real or imagined. No one likes to feel criticized.

In the same situation, we might be tempted to defend our initial statement by saying, "I am not the one who was late! Besides, we are talking about you, not me. I simply asked a question; why do you have to be so difficult?" Oops! Now this conversation has officially gone sideways thanks not just to your colleague's defensiveness, but to yours as well. When the other person responds defensively, you either shut the duck up or stay calm and clarify what you meant. You might say, "It wasn't my intention to question your work ethic. When you were late, I was concerned that something was wrong." Then embrace silence.

When people sense that their characters are being questioned, they tend to feel embarrassed or hurt, which causes them to react defensively. If they believe that we have said (or implied) that they are rude, inconsiderate, self-centered, unreliable, irresponsible, incompetent, etc., they will have a strong urge to protect themselves and their feelings of self-worth. For example, if we say, "Jane, you seem really distracted lately. Are you okay?" Jane may respond defensively by retorting, "I'm fine - but I am a busy mom and my time is not my own," or "Just try having as many balls in the air as I do," or "I can't believe you are giving me a hard time with everything I have going on!" Even with your relatively innocuous question, Jane may feel that her image as a reliable person is on the line and, to protect herself and her feelings of self-worth, she responds defensively.

When you're up against a situation like this, resist the urge to react. Stay focused on your ultimate goal for the conversation and be willing to immediately let any defensive comments go for the sake of staying on track. Instead of saying, "Sheesh! I was just trying to be nice. Don't you think you're overreacting?" try this: "Wow, it sounds like you have a lot on your plate right now. Is there anything I can do to support you?" You are far more likely to get a productive response if you avoid your own defensiveness even when the other person is getting defensive.

Even when the stakes don't seem high at all, like with the "are you okay" or "what's up" questions above (or my salad dressing incident), many of us are quick to defend ourselves. When the stakes *are* high, defensiveness is all the more likely, so just accept that no matter how perfectly crafted your message is, people may still respond defensively. As soon as you do, you can start working on choosing not to react to defensiveness and instead to simply let it run its course.

Hitting a Soft Spot

If you confront somebody with the "straight goods" and he or she responds defensively, there is a good chance that you have touched on a sensitive issue. In other words, there may actually be some truth in what you are saying. For example, if somebody says to me that she believes I need to speak up to be heard and that I am just too darn quiet, I would be surprised by the comment (since I am a little, shall we say, talkative), yet I would not feel defensive because I am confident in my belief that I am an outspoken person. On the other hand, if she had said to me that I need to learn to control how much I talk because other people feel that they can't get a word in edgewise when I am around, then I would be far more likely to respond defensively because on some level I already know that my talkativeness is not always constructive.

One year, a secretary of mine gave feedback to my boss for my annual performance review, saying that I was disorganized (which is a "hot" term). As you can easily imagine, I was quite defensive about this feedback and immediately turned the tables on her. I claimed that *she* was the disorganized one, then I threw in some extra criticism for good measure: she was always wasting my precious time talking to me about her personal problems. I reacted this way because I like to think of myself as an organized person but really, if I had been completely honest with myself, I would have admitted that on some level, my secretary was right. I do tend to be somewhat disorganized.

When you address people's shortcomings - or even when you simply explain your feelings without actually pointing any fingers of blame - you can expect defensive reactions because you know you'll likely be hitting a nerve. Those soft spots aren't something you can control and they shouldn't prevent you from having your tough talk. Just knowing they are there and understanding where a defensive reaction may be coming from is a good way to help prevent you from reacting unproductively to defensive responses.

Defensiveness: an Attempt to Undermine Your Perspective

Remember, when people start denying things, making excuses, justifying poor behavior or blaming others, it is a big flashing warning sign that they are on the defensive - big time. These reactions are people's misguided attempts to convince you as well as themselves that they are blameless. Defensiveness is a desperate attempt to rewrite the truth. They are hoping that if they keep saying something is true, somehow it will be. Of course, the more they protest or try to convince you, the less convinced you become. The reality is that a defensive response does the opposite of what it sets out to do: it undermines rather than bolsters credibility. We are left wondering why they don't just have the courage to own up to the truth. Unless one of you chooses not to get involved in the cycle of defensive retaliations, your discussion will quickly become a "win or lose" scenario in which both parties compete to set the record straight. Your talk becomes frenzied as each person picks apart the other's flawed defensive arguments until there is nothing left but raw emotions and flared tempers.

"In conflict, defensiveness is like blood in the water to a shark. A little here, a little there, and in no time the situation has degenerated into a feeding frenzy."

- James W. Tamm[20]

Rather than fan the flames by reacting to defensive comments and picking apart "untruths" or skewed stories, it is best to let the other person's defensiveness simply fizzle out naturally. Once he or she is finished speaking, you will have the opportunity to respond powerfully. There is no need to wrestle with the other person's defensive reactions and there is no chance that anything you could say in retaliation would be productive, anyway.

Your Skills in Action: Defensive Don

Let's look at an example of how to handle defensiveness in a tough workplace conversation: Imagine you have a colleague, Don, who loves to joke and have fun. Most of the time you are okay with it, but every once in a while he goes just a bit too far. In your last meeting, when you were suggesting certain accommodations for your upcoming conference in Vegas, Don snorted, "Ugh, you are such a princess. You don't *always* have to stay in a five-star resort, you know." Everyone snickered and your face turned the color of a tomato. You offered a small laugh, but wisely said nothing. Inside, you are really upset and, after a short cooling-off period, you decide to talk to Don.

At an appropriate time and place, you deliver your message:

> "Don, when you called me a princess in the meeting this morning, I felt really embarrassed. If you have an issue with my suggestion of where to stay for the conference, I have no problem discussing that. I just have a problem with being called a princess." STOP TALKING (and prepare for a defensive response).

Defensive Don responds by saying, "Aw, come on, Diane! I was just having some fun with you. Why don't you lighten up and take the comment in the context in which it was intended?"

Does Don's response make you feel better or convince you that you don't know how to take a joke? Nope! What Don is doing is trying to convince you (and himself too) that he did not make the joke at your expense. He is not a mean-spirited guy, after all. To accomplish this, Defensive Don casts the blame on you for taking his comments the wrong way. It is really tempting to react and say something like, "Hey, I know how to take a joke, but you always take things too far!" or "Don't tell me I need to lighten up! *You* need to learn a thing or two about respect and appropriate behavior at work!" These kinds of reactions will only elicit more defensive responses that could spiral into a big blowout and a seriously damaged working relationship.

So, how can you respond powerfully in a way that sticks to the facts and gets your point across without antagonizing Don further? How about:

> "It may not have been your intention to embarrass me, but that was the impact. I thought you deserved to know." STOP TALKING (short and sweet!).

Now, zip it up! Choose not to say anything further. Notice that your comments convey no blame or shame. You are taking ownership of your experience and not casting judgment on Don for his comments. You avoid retaliating against his defensive comments, which helps wind the discussion down more quickly.

Plus, you come out of the conversation looking both reasonable and confident. Not too shabby!

Okay, but what if Defensive Don flat-out denies calling you a princess in that meeting? What if he says that he would never, ever say anything like that? Would you now be convinced that you are hearing things or that you must have had a psychotic episode? I don't think so. Instead, you are likely to be even more upset and irritated because now Don has added insult to injury with his denial.

Unfortunately, saying, "I know what I heard, you weasel!" or accusing him of being a liar will only get you into a heated (and childish) yes-you-did-no-I-didn't circular debate that will never go anywhere. No matter how annoyed you are, take a quick mental dump and say this instead:

> "I am happy to talk about the issue of where we should stay at the conference. What you deserve to know is that I was offended by the comments you made about me at the meeting."

Stop there. End of story. You have made your point and do not have any need to engage further. There is no need to accuse anyone of lying; whether Don remembers what he said or not, now he knows that you aren't okay with those kinds of comments, which was your only real goal for this conversation.

What Not to Do...

We are often tempted when someone responds defensively to jump into the content of the excuse, explanation or justification. However, because defensive reactions often equate to people grasping at straws, if you indulge those comments by responding to their content, you almost guarantee that your conversation will veer way off course. Dealing with another person's defensiveness is not only aggravating and upsetting, it is exhausting. Imagine if, during my performance review, my boss had engaged in the content of my remarks about my secretary being disorganized and too chatty. The issue of *her* performance was completely off topic because we were supposed to be talking about *my* performance. Instead, what he did (which was very effective) was acknowledge my perspective and put himself in my shoes. He said something along the lines of: "It sounds like it is upsetting for you to have someone describe you as 'disorganized.' Do you think there is any validity in what she said?" After a little huffy fit, I was ready to get back on track and discuss what I could do to be more organized and efficient in my practice. My boss stayed focused on his goal for this tough talk and it paid off for all concerned. Take a page from my boss' book and resist the temptation to wade into a person's excuses or justifications. They will only serve to derail your conversation - not what you want after all of your hard work and preparation.

Here is another example that many of us can relate to: Think about how many times you have heard a million-and-one excuses for why someone is late. You know, the alarm didn't go off, there was an accident on the bridge, the dog got sick, someone took the car keys. Very often, the temptation is to provide some solutions as if we were talking to our children, like, "Why don't you buy a new alarm clock?" or "Maybe if you got up 15 minutes earlier?" Uh oh - what we have done here is validate these lame excuses for being late. Trust me, other people do not need any help from you; their own stories will surpass anything you can dream up! Now the conversation has drifted way off track, and you are probably getting more and more agitated because now you are talking about the best places to buy a cool, tricked-out alarm clock instead of the actual problem, which was (oh, right) the other person's lateness.

Instead of helping the other person justify his or her actions (and validate the defensiveness), you simply need to listen, then acknowledge that he or she has had a number of challenges being on time. Then, once it is your turn to speak again, calmly repeat your expectations. Here's how:

> "I understand that things do come up from time to time. What I have noticed is a pattern of you being late. My expectation is that you will be at work on time, so you need to plan accordingly." STOP TALKING.

There; that's all you need to say. If the other person reiterates his or her excuses, you will simply need to reiterate your expectations. Stay calm and avoid getting sucked into the drama of defensiveness in order to keep your talk on track.

Cut Them Some Slack

Understanding *why* people react defensively can take the sting out of any hurtful or upsetting things they say out of defensiveness, which can in turn prevent us from reacting or responding in kind. We want to pay attention to them, even if they are responding defensively, and acknowledge their concerns and points of view. By doing so, you maintain an atmosphere of respect, which allows people to save face and provides time for the message to sink in. Acknowledging or finding some truth in what a person on the defensive is saying can be very disarming. Remember to cut the other person the same slack you would cut yourself (or maybe even more if you are exceptionally hard on yourself). For example, if we say something that hurts someone, we might say, "I was provoked; I had no choice! Anyone would do what I did," rather than beating ourselves up for our actions. We mess up at times and so do our colleagues. Forgiving others both for their actions and for their defenses goes a long way in ensuring that your conversations will have successful outcomes.

Let's put our new tools to work and see how we can listen through a defensive reaction in some workplace situations.

Dealing With a Breach of Trust: Gossiping Gloria

Imagine your surprise when you find out that something you said in confidence to your coworker, Gloria, has not only come back to you but now the story has taken on a whole new, ugly twist. While out for lunch, you had told Gloria that you were frustrated with the time it was taking to get advice from Human Resources because you had a situation that you needed to deal with urgently and your hands were tied until they got back to you. Your inside voice leaked out and you said, "Aren't we essentially their clients? Aren't they supposed to be serving us? It ticks me off that we always have to wait for them!"

The next thing you know, you are getting the cold shoulder from your friends in HR and you are still waiting for the advice you need. When you ask them what's going on, you find out that the HR department is in an uproar. They have heard that you think they are doing a terrible job and are obviously very upset. You feel sick about what has happened and you have apologized to them. Now, you have to talk to Gloria. You have put it off for awhile and are at the point where you can't even look Gloria in the eye anymore. It's definitely time to talk.

You are clear that right now your relationship with Gloria is at stake. You really feel like you can no longer trust her, which is a problem because you work very closely together. You want to let Gloria know how you are feeling and clear the air. It feels to you like she is getting away with something. All of this worrying and obsessing about the conversation is consuming you; you haven't had a decent night's sleep for a week and are having a hard time focusing at work. As part of your preparation for this conversation, you anticipate how Gloria is going to react when you deliver your message. You are sure that she will be defensive or deny that she said anything to anyone, or she may tell you that what she said had been misinterpreted. Feeling prepared, you arrange to speak to her.

Here is one way to approach your conversation:

"Gloria, the HR department has not gotten back to me with that urgent advice I needed. When I called to inquire, I got a very cool reception and they informed me that they were very upset at me for saying that they were not doing a good job. You are the only person I talked to about my concerns. I am really upset that you shared something I told you in confidence." STOP TALKING. (Resist the urge to keep yapping!)

You then zip it up and wait; you are ready for a defensive reaction - and react she does! Gloria predictably denies saying anything to HR; then she changes her story to say that HR had misinterpreted what she had said and gives you her version of events. You listen closely and stay silent. Gloria then tries to convince you that she is not the type of person who would leak a secret. Are you convinced? Of course not! You listen calmly and, once Gloria is finished, you say:

"No matter what your intent was or what you actually said to HR, I want you to know that the result is that my relationship with HR has been negatively affected and my trust in you is shaken."

There is nothing more to say to Gloria at this point. You have made your point and rubbing her nose in it now would only serve to send any positive results of your tough talk up in smoke. It is unnecessary and unproductive to point out that Gloria switched her story or accuse her of being a shameless gossip because it would likely embarrass her and potentially spur even more defensive reactions. By allowing Gloria to save face despite her defensiveness, your message gets heard loud and clear.

Delivering Sensitive News: Dress-Down Debbie

Imagine you supervise staff members who work with the public. There is no formal dress code, but you do feel that casual jeans and runners is taking comfort too far. Most of your employees seem to understand this instinctively, but one employee, Dress-Down Debbie, persists in wearing baggy, faded jeans and grass-stained tennis shoes to work on a daily basis. It isn't that she's doing a bad job, but you feel that her attire does not portray your organization in a professional light to her customers.

In a private meeting, you let Debbie know that you think her attire is inappropriate for dealing with the public and you would like her to dress more professionally. Debbie reacts defensively and tells you that by being casual, she comes across as more "relatable" to her clients. She goes on to tell you that people should not judge others by how they dress. You are a bit irritated and feel like blurting out, "Look, Debbie, you can't come to work looking like you are just about to do some gardening!" You resist the urge, however, and instead put yourself in her shoes (even if they are grubby) and acknowledge her perspective. Here's how:

> "Debbie, it sounds like you believe that dressing casually makes you more approachable for clients and you don't think others should tell you how to dress. I have a different perspective. I believe that wearing jeans and running shoes does not set the kind of professional image that we want. It may not seem fair, but my expectation is that you will not wear jeans or running shoes to work again." STOP TALKING.

Debbie then whines that she is on her feet all day and deserves to be comfortable. You agree that she should be comfortable but you hold firm that running shoes and jeans do not fit the bill. You understand that comfort is important to her - hey, it's important to you, too - but she will have to find more suitable apparel that also gives her the comfort she wants at work. By reiterating your point in a way that is calm and concise, you communicate confidence in your message - and that helps Debbie get the picture as quickly as possible, regardless of her personal opinions on the matter. Remember, you don't have to try to change her mind - you just have to communicate your expectations.

These were just a few examples of how to listen through another person's defensive reaction without getting caught up in the drama and potentially contributing to a long, unpleasant, unproductive conversation or starting the next world war. You *can* listen without agreeing or giving up on what is important to you. Remember, you don't want to get caught up in a defensive reaction or you will likely end up scratching your head, wondering how you got so off track and how your message got lost in the shuffle. Ensure you are heard in the *first* conversation by avoiding indulging the other person's defensiveness from the get-go. Once you can do that, you no longer have to worry about how to handle a defensive reaction; they will simply fizzle out on their own.

A Final Caution

As I was learning more about defensiveness, I started to talk to my family and friends about it and what I quickly learned was that telling someone that they are being defensive is universally the fastest way to cause an intense and immediate defensive flare-up. The only person you need to remind not to be defensive is *you*; you cannot change other people (and you don't have to in order to communicate your message), so please don't try.

When somebody else is being defensive, I know that I have a challenge on my hands; it is time to shut the duck up and pay attention to the other person, no matter what I think about what is being said. When I listen without judgment, I help the other person save face, especially if he or she might feel embarrassed by the conversation. I also remind myself that when the defensiveness fizzles out, I will have an opportunity to respond powerfully. Listening to a person's defensive rant does not mean you are agreeing with it; you are simply being smart about how to manage the conversation. When we listen despite the other person's reaction, the conversation will wrap up much more quickly and go a whole lot more smoothly.

Top Tools to Recall: Dealing With Defenses

- ✔ Be prepared for a defensive reaction so you don't get caught off guard.
- ✔ Know that the other person has reasons for responding defensively. Help him or her save face by embracing silence, paying attention and listening.
- ✔ No matter how tempted you are, avoid reacting in kind or getting caught up in their excuses, justifications, blaming, whining, etc.
- ✔ Keep your primary goal in the forefront of your mind - it will help you to resist the urge to react to the details.
- ✔ When the other person's defensiveness fizzles out, you will have an opportunity to respond powerfully, I promise.

Excellent - now that you have chosen to sidestep the other person's defensive reaction, you may be at the stage where you can wrap things up. Remember, however, that not all of your conversations will go this smoothly (or if they do, please tell me your secret!). Despite your best efforts, sometimes people have unexpectedly strong reactions: yelling, sobbing, begging, threatening... the list goes on. This puts a whole new pressure on you that goes beyond the average defensive response, but don't worry: you are just a few page turns away from getting the tools you need for even the craziest of reactions.

Tame the Elephant in the Office
(in 4 pretty easy steps)

Step 1: Prepare to Talk

Get clear about what the real issue is and write it down in three sentences or less. Then determine what your ultimate goal is for the conversation. Be realistic.

Step 2: Design and Deliver Your "ABC Message"

What do you say and how do you say it? It's as easy as "ABC:" make it Accurate, Brief and Clear. Don't waste your time dancing around the issue; be honest and give people the "straight goods" in a way that is respectful and nonjudgmental.

Step 3: Stop Talking and Start Listening

Once you have delivered your ABC message, listen without interruption to hear the other person out. This may be your toughest challenge, but it is essential to keep the conversation on track... and it is easier than you think!

Step 4: Respond Powerfully

This is your opportunity to respond (not react) and clarify in a way that is confident, concise and clear. No excuses. No justifications. No blame.

Chapter 10:

Managing Freak-Outs

Chapter highlights:

- ☐ *Fight the urge to fight, flee or fold from the conversation when the other person has a nasty blowup.*
- ☐ *Ignore your instincts (just this once!).*
- ☐ *Diffuse talking time bombs: be calm, be quiet, be present.*

If you thought dealing with defensiveness was tricky, well, get ready for an even bigger challenge when people have even stronger reactions: blowups, tear-fests, shameless begging, insult-slinging or threats. The other person has gone beyond the garden variety reaction - defensiveness - and is doing what I tactfully like to call "freaking out." When this happens, anticipated or not, it's important to have the confidence that we can handle the other person's reaction *and* keep our cool so that our tough conversations end up with successful outcomes.

Just like with defensiveness, we must remember not to fuel the other person's fire. In tense conversations, the fuel is our negative reactions to the other person's freak-outs. You must choose your responses wisely, which can be challenging - but not impossible - when the other person is having a strong emotional reaction.

Basic Instincts

Our most primal of protective instincts tell us to fight, flee or fold when staring down the barrel of a freak-out. When a freak-out occurs, it's really easy to have those instincts triggered and react before we even realize what is going on. In challenging conversations, it is never a good idea to go with your basic instincts. When these instincts are triggered, the blood that our brains desperately need to think through the situation clearly and objectively is diverted to our large running muscles. This was great for our ancestors, who had to either flee from predators or fight them, but it is not very helpful in a tense conversation when we need a higher level of brain function.

"A life of reaction is a life of slavery, intellectually and spiritually. One must fight for a life of action, not reaction."

- Rita Mae Brown[21]

So what exactly are our triggers? Well, they may be comments from the other person that call into question our fairness, competence, commitment, integrity, trustworthiness, character, etc. Basically, when someone has a strong emotional reaction to our message, it is more than natural for these triggers to be set off because we want to defend ourselves not only against the content of what is being said but also against the craziness of the freak-out we are now being confronted with.

Fight, Flee or Fold

Let's look at the framework of the three "Fs" that can undermine our ability to successfully hang in there through our tough talks and see them through to a desirable conclusion. We have made it this far, so we sure don't want to give up now!

Fight

Most of us manage to fight our basic instincts for a time. However, as the other person's emotional reaction intensifies with jarring remarks, threats, shouting or anything else that triggers us, we become convinced that we can't take the pressure anymore and end up blurting out some accusatory, critical or otherwise unhelpful response. Staying cool here is like trying to stay cool in a sauna. In the "fight" frame of mind, our blood starts boiling and our carefully thought out goal for the conversation vanishes before our very eyes. We've lost our cool and go from hoping to achieve a productive result to wanting to win, prove someone wrong, get back at someone, protect ourselves or defend our points of view.

If you ply other people with any combination of techniques to "win the battle," their emotions will escalate, which will only intensify their attacks. Allowing ourselves to fall into fight mode means that nothing gets solved while both parties become more and more entrenched in their perspectives or points of view. Both people become increasingly more convinced about how right they are and how absolutely wrong the other person is. This is not a great plan for any tricky conversation because it leads to a vicious attack-counterattack cycle.

Our drive to fight is one of our basic instincts and has been reinforced by all of those Hollywood action movies we love to watch. Unfortunately, in real life our basic instinct to fight is usually counterproductive and does not get us the results we are hoping for. Hollywood has led us astray here big time!

My Fight Story: Ineffectual Ed

Many years ago, I was involved in a business in which one of the bosses hired a management/financial expert to provide business advice. Over time, it became apparent to me that this "expert," whom I'll call "Ineffectual Ed," was not only charging us exorbitant fees, but the reports and information he was providing were riddled with glaring mistakes. I was obviously not seeing his value in the business. I tried on a number of occasions to ask Ineffectual Ed questions about his advice and fees, but he would always give me the runaround (one thing he *was* very effective at doing). I finally spoke to the boss about my concerns and my recommendation was that we no longer do business with Ed. The boss wanted proof that Ed was not doing a good job; he thought Ed was a nice guy and was not comfortable firing him without giving him an opportunity to explain himself. In fact, what he really wanted was for me to sit down with Ineffectual Ed to itemize my concerns and point out all of the errors in the reports he had prepared. Ugh. Talk about a dreaded conversation!

I meticulously prepared the facts and figures for the meeting with Ed and the boss. I was going to be in the hot seat and I knew it. But now, I felt sorry for the guy, too. I wouldn't want to be on the receiving end of a talk like this! I anticipated that he might freak out; after all, I was calling into question both his competence and his integrity. During the conversation, I calmly pointed out my concerns one by one as we went through my notes. Ed spent a great deal of time justifying his numbers, his expertise and the value he brought to the business. When that did not work, he finally lost his cool and accused me of not knowing what I was doing. "You don't have any financial expertise, do you, Diane?" he fumed. "I don't think you really get how businesses run!"

Had Ed just questioned my intelligence? Had he just questioned my competence as a businesswoman? You bet he had - and I got my back up immediately. Now the fight was on. Didn't he know I had a university degree in commerce, not to mention I had graduated with honors? I barked that I could plainly see the errors in his numbers and that he was committing highway robbery with his fees. Did he think I was stupid? I had plenty of business experience and I told Ineffectual Ed all about it - so maybe he was the one who didn't know what he was doing! Now, I wanted him to admit the error of his ways and I was more than happy to take the gloves off and rant and rave until he did. Suffice it to say the whole thing was very ugly: we hurled insults and shouted over each other until we were both red in the face.

In the end, we did stop working together, but the result could have been the same without so much wasted time and so many hard feelings if I had not reacted and thrown myself into fight mode when Ed had questioned my competence (clearly a hook for me!). Yes, Ed had "started it" with an attack, but I counterattacked - and that's when things started to spiral out of control. If I had been able to keep my cool, then Ineffectual Ed would have been able to save face, at least a little. I would have been way better off putting myself in his shoes (empathy) to realize how humiliating the whole situation must have been for him. Defending myself and going on the attack created a *very* uncomfortable meeting and made me look pretty mean-spirited. It was an unnecessarily messy end to our working relationship.

Flee

If that whole "fight" scenario sounds like a totally unfamiliar nightmare to you, you might be a "fleer," someone whose instinct is to run from the conversation as fast as possible when things heat up. Many of us are experts in the art of fleeing, having any of the following tricks up our sleeves:

- ✗ *Swift subject changes*, as in: "Okay, now that you know about your demotion, can we just talk about the Brooks project?" You may be inclined to change the subject when you are uncomfortable and hoping that by talking about something else, you both will be able to just "move on." Yeah, right. Don't you think the other person might have a thing or two to say about his demotion? Wouldn't you?

- ✗ *Abrupt endings*, such as: "I'm sorry, this conversation is over. I am not prepared to discuss it any further." I don't know about you, but when someone tells me a conversation is over, I am usually determined to keep it going and I will resort to dirty tactics if necessary. People don't take "no" for an answer well when they don't feel that they have had an opportunity to be heard. Don't forget that you are supposed to be turning the conversation over and really listening!

- ✗ *Physically exiting the conversation*, for example: "Sorry to be so rude, but I just remembered I have to get this file to the courier by 2:30. I'll be back in a sec." Then - oops! - we cleverly get "sidetracked" and never return. The other person isn't fooled and is annoyed that we did not have the courtesy or the courage to finish the discussion. (I will never forget when one of my relatives called to ask how I was. It had been a difficult day and I started to share some of my frustration. I was stopped mid-sentence and told, "Okay, dear, that's nice. Talk to you soon." Then there was a click on the other end of the line. It felt like I had had a door shut in my face!)

- ✗ *Emotionally exiting the conversation*. This is a tricky tactic: On the outside you appear calm, cool and collected, but the reality is that you would rather be walking over hot coals than continue this conversation. So you "check out," suddenly becoming very interested in shuffling papers on your desk, mentally packing for your next vacation or maybe silently humming your favorite show tunes. Don't think this goes unnoticed because trust me, it doesn't.

Fleeing can give you some sense of control and relief in the short term, but it really creates more problems in the long run. By fleeing, what you are really conveying is, "I am uncomfortable with your freak-out or reaction, so this conversation has officially ended." When you take a stand like this, you have pretty much guaranteed that your conversation is *not* over and ensured the necessity of a follow-up conversation (or two or ten). Why? First, everyone wants to be heard and understood. It is a basic human need. Second, nobody wants to be told what to do or how things are going to go down. People defiantly respond to your flight and may even hunt you down later to force you to talk to them.

Whether your conversation continues right then (despite your attempt to end it) or later down the road, fleeing because the other person has had a strong reaction to your message will likely intensify his or her attack or otherwise escalate the behavior that you found intolerable in the first place. Just think of the last time you saw a mother trying to say "no" to her three-year-old at the checkout in a grocery store; don't expect that your difficult conversation will go any differently! Unless you set the stage for communication, you can expect toddler-like temper tantrums, crocodile tears, the silent treatment, pouting, you name it.

Even if the other person seems to be fine with your untimely end to the conversation, don't be so sure; chances are that the person's indignation will go underground, creating all sorts of havoc. Remember my boss who scolded me for my inept research and then abruptly dismissed me like a poorly prepared school girl? He obviously thought it was over - but I certainly didn't! My troubles with him boiled beneath the surface and I had plenty to say about him and his behavior to anyone who would listen. The bottom line is that when you flee a tough talk, all you are doing is delaying the inevitable (i.e. the remainder of your conversation).

Fold

Imagine the person you are having the conversation with responds with shouting, insults, pleading, flattery (otherwise known as sucking up) or maybe even threats in an attempt to convince you to retreat or change your mind. The pressure is killing you and you would love nothing more than for this tough talk to just end already. When you are under the gun, sometimes the only way you see to get some relief is to relent, back down or fold. Unfortunately, what you are actually doing when you choose to fold is either slinking away like a badly behaved pet (when really, you have no reason to feel that way) or giving in like the mom at the grocery store who caves and buys the candy bar just to get her kid to stop screaming.

"An appeaser is one who feeds a crocodile, hoping it will eat him last."

- Sir Winston Churchill

The biggest problem when we fold, especially in the face of a freak-out, is that we end up rewarding the very behavior that made us so uncomfortable in the first place. Imagine you had folded with Weekend Wanda from chapter one (the one with your granny coming for a visit), after she had begged and then flattered and then threatened you, even though you had already taken the time off well in advance. Wanda would have learned that by putting the screws into you, she could get you to do whatever she wanted, which would obviously set you up for more problems down the road.

Another problem with folding is that it is cumulative: it just gets easier and easier to fold each time you do it and in very short order, the other person comes to expect it. I think about how many times I have folded with my kids; no wonder they see my bold statements about consequences as idle threats! So, why are we tempted to fold when we know that we are ultimately just shooting ourselves in the foot? One of the main reasons is that we feel some relief because the other person is ecstatic to be off the hook and the conversation can feel like it's over. Think about a time when you wanted to say "no" to someone. The other person begs and pleads for what feels like an eternity and finally, out of sheer exhaustion, you relent. Sure, that makes the other person happy - they got their way! But how do *you* feel? Maybe you're glad that the conversation is over, but now you've made a commitment that you never wanted in the first place. And do you get treated like a hero for saying "yes?" Maybe for awhile, but you can bet that the next time that person needs someone to do something, you will be the first person that gets called.

I think that most of us have been there at some point. When we back down, we feel backed into a corner. We resent the other person for being so persistent. We tell ourselves that not only is this crappy new situation not our fault, it is really all *their* fault! The more we think about it, the more upset we become. We tell ourselves that we didn't fold because we wanted to; it was because they *made* us fold with their threats or tears or begging.

While it does make perfect sense to blame someone else for the way a conversation ended, especially when they were freaking out at you, it's far more productive to look at yourself in the mirror and reflect upon the role you played. The big cost of folding is that it affects our relationships at work, not to mention the personal relationships that our discontent spills into as well as our own sense of self-respect. (If you find yourself in this position, remember that the two-minute whine rule is your friend. Complain for two minutes to someone you trust. Get it off your chest and then figure out a way to work things out.)

Facing a Freak-Out: Nightmare Nanny

Remember that folding or otherwise backing down is not going to solve the overarching problem that led you to have your conversation in the first place, even if it does give you the illusion of relief in the short term. If you do back down, you risk shifting the balance in your working relationships, which is especially problematic if you are in a supervisory or managerial role.

Put yourself in this scenario: You are a busy working mom with two kids and an office to run. Your kids are young and you've hired someone to come into your home to look after them while you're at work. One evening, after a loooong day at the office, you come home to find the nanny watching TV. In her defense, the youngest is napping and the oldest is at a play date, but your inside voice is seething: "She is well paid. Why isn't she doing the laundry, ironing or cleaning up in the kitchen?" You start to feel resentful because in your mind, you are a caring employer. You let her take your kids to visit her friends, run personal errands and do her shopping - all in your car. Friends have told you that you are way too nice and now you are starting to agree.

In an effort to make your nanny get the picture, you have left hints about laundry, dishes and the messy kitchen. You had hoped that would be direct enough, but your hints have obviously been too subtle because she seems oblivious to your concerns and happily flips on the TV whenever the kids don't require her attention. Finally, you muster up the courage to talk about the issue. After crafting what you hope will be a great ABC message, you start the conversation well, telling her your expectations and some of the chores that you would like done.

To your surprise, your nanny suddenly and unexpectedly has a complete meltdown. She starts sobbing and accuses you of questioning her integrity. She says that it is her job to look after your children and she takes that responsibility very seriously. If you want help with the house, she says haughtily, you should hire a maid. You are stunned by her reaction, but what can you do? You need her; childcare is in high demand and you're afraid of what might happen if she quits.

So you fold. In fact, you crumple. Where is the tough, no-nonsense manager you play so well by day? You end up apologizing for your "unreasonable" expectation that she do housework. Then you tell her how grateful you are to have her. You contemplate offering to upgrade your cable package so she could enjoy her downtime even more. In short, the whole scene is pretty pathetic. Now, you have set the precedent that all your nanny has to do is shed a few tears and not only will you back down, but you will even go out of your way to make it up her.

After the conversation, you are understandably upset. You blame your nanny for the outcome of your conversation, but *you* are the one who lost sight of your goal and caved. Because you folded, there has been a distinct shift in power in your working relationship, even though *you* are the employer.

What went wrong? How could you have responded more productively? The conversation could have gone a little like this:

"I appreciate that your priority is the children and that you take your role seriously. They are very important to me as well. I would also appreciate you doing a few chores when the baby is sleeping. Your help would make spending time with my children much easier for me when I get home." STOP TALKING.

To really make your message stick and bolster your confidence, make sure you have your backup plan in place. It would be a shame to lose your nanny, sure, but chances are she doesn't want to lose her well-paid, perk-filled job as much as you don't want to have to look for a replacement. Don't be intimidated into folding, either by someone else's threats or your own fears of what might happen. Come up with a backup plan that works for you so you can stick to your guns and not fold under pressure.

Battle Your Basic Instincts

We now know our basic instincts are not likely to help us when they are triggered by another person's emotional meltdown. If we respond by fighting, fleeing or folding, we will invariably make things worse. If you get caught up in the heat of the moment and are tempted to commit one of the three "Fs," ask yourself if you really want to fan the flames here - because that's what you are doing when you choose to indulge your basic instincts. Instead, give the other person some space to have the big, dramatic meltdown. Let the fire fizzle out. It works with defensiveness and it works with freak-outs, too - you just need a little more resolve.

Sure, you may be thinking, but *how*? There are a number of things you can do, but if you remember nothing else, remember this: do the opposite of what your instincts tell you to do. For those of you who are old enough to be *Seinfeld* fans, you may remember the episode "The Opposite," in which George Constanza, who is unemployed, has no money and lives with his parents, decides that every decision he has ever made has been wrong and every instinct he has ever had has been flawed. He is sharing this revelation with Elaine and Jerry in their favorite diner when Jerry suggests that if every instinct of his is wrong, then the opposite of those instincts would have to be right. George is intrigued and decides to do the opposite of what his instincts tell him to do and see what happens. The results were astounding: he lands a job with the New York Yankees, meets a beautiful woman, moves out of his parents' house and, most importantly, gains confidence![22]

Now, I am obviously not suggesting that all of your dreams will come true if you ignore your instincts, but believe me when I say it has been my experience that when I am in a tough talk that is getting heated, doing the opposite of what my instincts tell me has always been the right thing to do. Maybe it won't get me a job with the Yankees, but it really does help me accomplish my goals for my difficult conversations.

How Can You Diffuse Talking Time Bombs?

"Talking time bombs" is the term I like to use for conversations that turn ugly when the other person freaks out. Diffusing these time bombs isn't impossible as long as you are prepared. Here are some tools I use to help the freak-out fizzle out:

1. *Be Calm*

Is it hard to stay calm when someone is bawling like a child or screaming in your face? Do you want to put people in their place when you know they are telling bald-faced lies? Do you feel the pressure when someone is threatening your livelihood or insulting your intelligence? Of course! Staying calm can be hard, but hopefully it will be a little easier when you realize the power it has in your tough talks. Your calmness can be the antidote for another person's anger, frustration or sadness - no matter how melodramatic their freak-out. Stay calm and your conversation will be able to move on much more quickly.

2. *Be Quiet*

It's tough for people to continue freaking out if you don't keep adding fuel to the fire. If you aren't talking, you aren't using any "hot" language or reacting defensively to what is being said, so do yourself a favor and just shut the duck up. When our talks heat up, we are often tempted to say things along the lines of:

- ✗ Calm down!
- ✗ I think you are overreacting.
- ✗ Don't you think you are overreacting? (Even worse!)
- ✗ Cheer up. Things aren't that bad.
- ✗ Whoa, settle down there.

✗ I'm sorry that you are angry.

✗ I'm sorry you're so upset.

Can you imagine how you would react if someone said something like this to you when you were having your own freak-out? Would you calm down? I doubt it; I sure wouldn't! Not talking is one of the most efficient ways to diffuse a talking time bomb. When you feel like responding in any way, shape or form to a freak-out, *don't*. Instead, embrace silence and watch the flames die down before your eyes.

3. Be Present

It is critical that you remain present when people are freaking out at you. Don't fiddle with your electronics, turn away or sigh impatiently. If you are not paying attention, you will come across as disrespectful, which will only prolong the meltdown. Yes, even if they are being obnoxious or insanely unfair, you must stay present and do your best to listen without interrupting. It is about keeping your talk respectful, even if you feel in the heat of the moment that they don't deserve your respect. You are leading by example. Other people don't expect you to be respectful when they are freaking out so, when you *do* give them your careful attention, they are pleasantly surprised and unexpectedly disarmed, which calms them down much more quickly.

Remember my story about asking my hubby for more support so that I could better balance managing the household and developing my career? If you recall, I had anticipated that he would be upset and that his reaction might trigger my basic instincts. Those who know us best understand what "hooks" us... and when things heat up we don't always manage to resist the temptation. Hubby reacted as I had anticipated, but rather than wading in, arguing with him and blurting out comments I would later regret, I stayed present and chose to embrace silence. The results were incredible; the talking time bomb was diffused and the conversation moved to productive territory in record time (about 30 seconds). We were then able to have a problem-solving conversation in which, instead of feeling pitted one against the other, we were both on the same team.

"The most precious gift we can offer anyone is our attention..."

- Thich Nhat Hanh[23]

The bottom line is that the less you do or say in reaction to a freak-out, the faster the other person's reaction will fizzle out and the sooner you will have the opportunity to resume having a successful conversation. You may find the tools above easy to understand but difficult to put into practice, but I really encourage you to try. The more times you can put your new skills to work, the sooner they will feel like second nature.

See These Skills in Action: Ski Shortage

Here is a situation in which I was able to stifle my primary basic instinct, which is to fight like crazy. It was not a particularly high-stakes conversation, but it was one where I was able to avoid fueling the fire of a defensive reaction and reach a productive outcome as a result.

I was with my family at a fabulous ski resort. One beautiful, sunny Saturday, we decided that we wanted to skate ski for the day. When we arrived at the cross-country ski park, we were advised that it was very busy and we may not be able to get ski rentals. Hubby and I had our own gear but our kids did not. It was around 12:30pm so we decided to forge ahead, assuming that people would be bringing equipment back from their morning outings. The lodge was busy as expected, but a nice gentleman measured up our kids and said he had equipment for us. It was our lucky day... or so I thought!

Moments later, the fellow behind the desk yelled out across the room, "No, you cannot give the skis to those people [as if we didn't exist]! There are others ahead of them!" We were a little taken aback, as was the gentleman who was helping us. I went to speak to the fellow behind the desk to try to clarify. He informed me that it was the busiest day ever and he wasn't sure if we would get any equipment at all. I told him I wasn't trying to jump the queue, but I wanted to understand the system to ensure we had our names down when equipment came in from the morning skiers. He snippily informed me there was no system and barked out that he had no intention of creating one on the busiest day of the year.

I was starting to get a little irritated. I needed to calm myself so I wouldn't lose my cool. I swear I could almost *hear* my triggers getting pulled! Sure, he was probably out of line and maybe I could have justified calling him rude or disorganized. I could also go into "demanding lawyer mode" (which I do very well) and be hooked into a battle of wills with him. But I thought to myself,

Okay, what do I really want here and how am I most likely to get it? I wanted to get equipment and get out on this beautiful day. I did not want to ruin the rest of my afternoon by engaging in battle with this guy. Keep your eye on the prize, Diane, I told myself. I was not likely to get what I wanted by losing my cool. In fact, a freak-out would have almost certainly backfired based on his attitude thus far. I encouraged myself to remain respectful and polite and to try to find a way to be on his side.

I took a deep breath, then here is what I said:

> "I see you have a lot going on and I don't want to add to your stress. I am wondering what I can do to secure a spot in the queue without hovering."

He continued to be difficult for a few moments, repeating that he wasn't going to develop a system just for me today. I remained calm and I did not move from the desk - no fighting, fleeing or folding. Finally, he asked me to fill out a form and told me to go and have a coffee and they would call me when some skis came in. I obliged and to my pleasant surprise, he called 20 minutes later to let us know they had skis available for the kids. Hubby was very proud of me for remaining so calm; he even said, "Wow, that was awesome. I would have lost it with that guy!"

Yes, a lot of people would have lost it with a guy like that or whomever they're dealing with in a tough conversation - and it's easy enough to understand why. However, you have to keep in mind that you need a real, productive goal for your conversations and "sticking it to her" or "putting him in his place" just don't cut it. Sure, I could have indulged my basic instinct to fight with the ski rental guy, but what would it have gotten me? Probably nothing more than agitation, high blood pressure and a long day of whining. It certainly wouldn't have gotten us any skis! Instead, I chose to stay calm and present so that I could have a successful talk and a fun-filled afternoon of skiing with my family.

When you can feel your triggers getting wiggled, remember that you have much more power than you think. You just need to be aware and prepared so that you can avoid letting your basic instincts kick in. You can fight your battle or flee or fold from it - or you can decide to stay calm and aim for a productive conversation. You get to choose, so choose wisely.

Top Tools to Recall: Fizzling Out Freak-Outs

- ✔ Being prepared for a meltdown can take the sting out of it when it happens because you can be more detached.
- ✔ Be aware of how you feel during your difficult conversations so you don't fall victim to your basic instincts when you are feeling triggered.
- ✔ Remember your three "Fs:" you can't achieve your goals if you fight, flee or fold.
- ✔ Let the freak-out fizzle out by taking control and doing the opposite of what your instincts tell you to do. Be calm, quiet and present.

Sure, you may be thinking, I can see how this all works on paper, but what about when you're on the front lines? How are you supposed to fight your basic instincts and stay calm and attentive when the other person is standing right in front of you throwing the biggest freak-out of all time?

If you're concerned that your challenging conversations will require superhero-caliber levels of willpower, never fear: in the next chapter, we are going to talk about some handy tools I've learned (a lot of times the hard way) to help you stay calm and collected under pressure. These tools are important because they can give you the confidence that you truly can handle anything that gets thrown your way. Other people's freak-outs will be no match for your legendary ability to stay cool, I promise!

Tame the Elephant in the Office

(in 4 pretty easy steps)

Step 1: Prepare to Talk

Get clear about what the real issue is and write it down in three sentences or less. Then determine what your ultimate goal is for the conversation. Be realistic.

Step 2: Design and Deliver Your "ABC Message"

What do you say and how do you say it? It's as easy as "ABC:" make it Accurate, Brief and Clear. Don't waste your time dancing around the issue; be honest and give people the "straight goods" in a way that is respectful and nonjudgmental.

Step 3: Stop Talking and Start Listening

Once you have delivered your ABC message, listen without interruption to hear the other person out. This may be your toughest challenge, but it is essential to keep the conversation on track... and it is easier than you think!

Step 4: Respond Powerfully

This is your opportunity to respond (not react) and clarify in a way that is confident, concise and clear. No excuses. No justifications. No blame.

Chapter 11:

Tools to Stay Cool

Chapter highlights:

- ☐ *Understand that their reactions are never personal (despite what they say!).*
- ☐ *Practice the best "stay cool" strategies for you: breathe deeply, observe rather than participate, adopt a calming mantra and/or play the "name that hook" game.*[24]

In the last chapter you learned that it is best not to act on your basic instincts when the other person has a freak-out during your talk, but you might be wondering *how* you can possibly be calm, quiet and present when faced with such extreme behavior. Although your willpower and self-discipline will certainly help, they are not entirely enough; knowing some tools to stay cool is essential for keeping things on track. All of the strategies we are going to cover can be used singly or in a combination that works best for you. They will help you to counter your basic instincts, stop you from fighting, fleeing or folding and keep you focused on the bigger picture: your goal for the conversation.

Their Reactions Are Never Personal

I often have to remind myself that crazy reactions are not about me – they are always and 100% about the other person. When it feels like people are being disrespectful, attacking you or making accusatory comments, remind yourself that *it is not personal*. It can be tough to believe, but I promise it's true. A perceived personal attack is really about the other person desperately trying to deflect the "blame" over to you. Now is the time for you to give him or her some space and time to digest the news you've just delivered. Be the bigger person here. While the other person is taking that much-needed time, you can think about what tools you would like to use to keep your talk on track. It may feel unnatural and even painful at first, but it will pay off and save you time and probably some sleepless nights in the long run.

"Maybe you are the 'cool' generation. If coolness means a capacity to stay calm and use your head in the service of ends passionately believed in, then it has my admiration."

- Kingman Brewster, Jr.[25]

Tool #1: Take Some Deep Breaths

In the past, you might have dismissed deep breathing as something only used by those crunchy-granola yoga types... but there actually is some science to support that deep breathing is very calming and helps keep you grounded and in the present. As an added bonus, your oxygen-deprived brain loves the extra shot of O_2, which means you will be able to think more clearly. I often have to remind myself to breathe before I open my mouth. (Imagine how the dynamics of a Ross family dinner would change if we all took deep breaths before we started talking!)

Tool #2: Watch the Drama - Don't Participate

Almost all of us love drama. If we aren't hooked on a soap opera, then we love drama-filled stuff like *Grey's Anatomy* or *Breaking Bad* or *How I Met Your Mother* or any one of the zillions of reality TV shows. You can expect drama in your difficult conversations, too, although the stakes will be considerably higher. When we watch our favorite shows, the TV usually has our rapt attention, yet we are only observing the drama and not participating. Take a cue from your TV habits for your tough conversations: pay attention, but don't participate.

Think of a time when you've been out in public, say at a restaurant or coffee shop, when you could hear the couple at the next table arguing. You wouldn't dream of getting involved, but can't restrain yourself from eavesdropping. In these situations, it's easy to be objective because you are a casual observer and not emotionally involved. That is the kind of objectivity we want to strive for when things heat up in our own difficult conversations. It is tricky, but entirely possible. The key is to remember that the other person's reactions - even the giant freak-outs - are no more about you than that couple's argument taking place at the next table or the most recent episode of *The Young and the Restless.* Once you intrinsically understand that other people's reactions are *never* about you and *always* and *only* about them, it will be easier to practice not getting involved in the drama and instead simply watch it unfold then fizzle out from a safe distance.

Tool #3: Play "Name That Hook"

As an observer, it's easier to be on the lookout for the inevitable "hook," which is what other people throw out for you to react to when they aren't getting what they want. Be wary and be wise; they probably already know how to hook you and will even change the bait a few times if necessary. Your task is to be on the lookout for the hook and acknowledge it in your own mind. You could say to yourself, "That's interesting that he is trying to appeal to my sense of professionalism" or "That's interesting that she is trying to flatter me." I find playing the "name that hook" game prevents me from going for the bait, reacting and getting sucked into the drama. Instead of reacting to what has been said, I can simply notice it and swim on by.

Here are some pretty common hooks to be on the lookout for:

- ☐ *Flattery:* Imagine your boss begs you, "Nobody else does it like you! I just can't manage without you! If you quit, then it's possible the company may fold! Please, pretty please, can't you just agree to stay on the project just a little bit longer at least until you can train somebody else?" Doesn't he give you the same spiel every time you try to quit? Don't fall for this one!

  Instead, you identify the hook - appealing to your sense of responsibility - and respond powerfully by saying, "I am glad to know that you value my contributions, but I am not going to be working here anymore because I am moving on."

- ☐ *Threats or intimidation:* They may be subtle, but you know they are there. Your bully of a client says, "If you can't do this rush order, then I will have to go to your boss. You know I am one of the company's biggest clients and I think you might want to keep me happy." Of course, because you prepared for the conversation and anticipated your client's reaction, you have already spoken to your boss about having your back.

  You correctly identify the hook: your client is trying to scare you into doing what he wants with a threat. Now, you can confidently reply, "I'm sorry, but the answer is 'no.' If you would like to speak to my boss, here is her contact information."

- ☐ *I'm not the problem, you are! (or some variation):* Imagine you have a conversation with your loud coworker to let him know that when he speaks loudly on the phone, it disturbs you to the point of not being able to concentrate. He may respond by saying, "I am not sure what your problem is; nobody else seems to have any concentration issues. Am I to blame if you have ears like a dog?"

  You name the hook and say to yourself, *That's interesting that he is trying to blame me for this*. Then you say calmly, "I may indeed have sensitive hearing and I think you deserve to know when you talk on the phone it is very disturbing to me. I would appreciate it if you could keep your voice down."

- ☐ *Accusing you of bad intentions:* Imagine your sales rep says to you, "Why are you questioning my judgment on the terms I negotiated with the supplier? Is it because you lost the big Roscoe deal and you want to deflect attention away from yourself?"

  Here again, you recognize the hook - accusing you of looking for a scapegoat - and calmly respond, "It sounds like you are disappointed that we lost the Roscoe project. I am, too. It is a complicated and unfortunate situation, but I am not sure how it is connected to what we are talking about here. Please know that in the future I expect to be consulted about the proposed terms on a deal before you agree to them."

- ☐ *Questioning your character:* Let's say you talk to your coworker about his unfortunate habit of eating his smelly tuna sandwiches at his desk in the small cubicle you both share. He says, "Well, you eat at your desk sometimes too, but I never say anything! I am just not that petty. You really should chill out - I have a right to eat where I want."

  You see the hook - accusing you of pettiness - and respond, "You make a valid point. I will make an effort not to eat at my desk. The problem for me is the smell of the tuna. I would appreciate it if you ate strong smelling food in the lunchroom and I will do the same."

Tool #4: Adopt a Calming Mantra

A mantra is an age-old tool for focusing the mind that has recently recaptured the spotlight thanks to things like yoga and meditation becoming trendy. A mantra is simply a calming phrase that you repeat over and over to yourself. I have experimented with adopting a mantra and I find it very helpful. The idea is to come up with something you can chant silently to yourself when you feel yourself being triggered and don't want to fall prey to your basic instincts. Your mantra should focus on the positive rather than the negative because it is much easier to follow through on "doing" something than "not doing" something. For example, if I told you not to think about elephants - boom! - I know for sure you immediately have elephants on the brain. You get the picture: we are more likely to do the "don't" if that is what we focus on, so let's focus on a "do" instead. Here are some ideas for your positive mantra:

- ✔ Stay cool.
- ✔ Stay calm.
- ✔ Stay focused.
- ✔ That's interesting!
- ✔ I am up to the plate.
- ✔ Wow!
- ✔ I am in control.
- ✔ Embrace silence.
- ✔ Pay attention.
- ✔ Swim by the hook.

A word of caution: If you are alone, you can feel free to chant your mantra aloud, but be careful about uttering it in front of others during your tough talks. You may be able to get away with saying your mantra aloud once or twice, but if you keep repeating "that's interesting!" or "wow!" over and over in response to everything the other person says, you will quickly discover that your mantra can provoke even more freak-outs because you are coming across as glazed over and inattentive (like when you ask your kids while they're watching TV if their homework is finished and you get a very unconvincing "mmhmm" in reply). Fortunately, mantras do work even silently, so feel free to rinse and repeat as much as needed in your head.

My "Staying Cool" Story: Mr. Tough Guy

Here is my story of staying cool from back in my legal days, when another lawyer decided to take a "tough guy" approach to negotiating with me. I had received a settlement offer from Mr. Tough Guy that seemed completely out to lunch. I told my boss what I thought about the offer and he agreed with my assessment. We decided that we would not make any kind of counteroffer because it was early on in the case and we still had more information to gather.

I informed Mr. Tough Guy by mail that we did not accept his offer. He immediately followed up with a phone call, obviously agitated and pushing me to put some kind of counteroffer on the table. I stayed firm and declined his demands. Not surprisingly, he became even more upset and his reaction escalated until I could practically smell the smoke coming out of his ears through the telephone receiver. He was shouting so loudly and for so long that I actually put the phone down and updated my workout schedule while he ranted and raved - and I could still hear every word. Luckily, I had the confidence to stay cool (talking to my boss before the call helped) and, once his tirade was over, I calmly repeated that we would not be making any counteroffer at this time. He huffed and puffed and his last words to me before he slammed down the phone were that I would "be sorry" - an empty threat.

"People who fly into a rage always make a bad landing."

- Will Rogers

The bottom line was that his combative tactics only served to undermine what he was hoping to achieve: a timely and lucrative settlement. When he started to raise his voice and carry on, I played "name that hook" and said to myself, "Oh, interesting. He is trying to intimidate me with shouting and threats because he is feeling desperate. I am in the driver's seat here and I choose not to react to his tactics." As he went on (and on and on), I also repeated a calming mantra to myself: "Swim by that hook, Diane! Don't bite!"

My mantra and my "name that hook" game kept me on track so that I didn't indulge any urges to retaliate or give in to his demands. Did Mr. Tough Guy get what he wanted? Nope! In fact, his antics gave me more resolve to hold my ground. I was calm, quiet and present and was able to reiterate our decision not to counteroffer without fighting, fleeing or folding.

What to Do if You Can't Handle the Heat

If you are really uncomfortable with something the other person has said, there are some things you can do - but first, remember that using "hot" language or getting defensive won't work. Avoid saying things like:

✗ Don't talk to me like that.

✗ How dare you speak to me like that?!

✗ You have no right to say that to me!

Statements like these will only serve to get the other person more worked up, even if you feel justified in saying them. (If you don't believe me, just try one of them out the next time you are in a heated conversation with your spouse, snippy colleague or mother... but don't say I didn't warn you!). Instead, try employing one of the following tactics:

1. *Exit the conversation in the heat of the moment.*

In the previous chapter, I emphasized how important it is to *not* flee from your difficult conversations. Here, exiting the conversation and fleeing are not the same thing as long as you are transparent and actually tell the other person what you are doing. Here are some examples of what you might say:

✓ I am feeling really reactive right now and I think that if we carry on, I might say or do something I will regret. I am going to take a few minutes here to cool down.

✓ I am trying really hard to stay with you here but I am starting to feel defensive. I am going to take a break.

✓ It seems like we are getting into dangerous territory. I believe we need to take a break.

In the circumstances above, you have been working at your conversation and now are letting the other person know you are you are not coping well in the moment. Your message is honest and transparent - the signs of a great ABC message - with no trace of avoidance or flight.

2. *Go back and address how you were spoken to at a later time.*

When I say "later," I really mean it. Wait until you are calm, cool and collected (and hopefully when the other person is too). Then, when you are ready, address any inappropriate comments calmly and without judgment. Here are some examples:

- ✔ Last week, when you called me a "raving lunatic," I felt humiliated.
- ✔ In our conversation the other day, when you told me that I needed to get my act together, I was really embarrassed.
- ✔ I was upset yesterday when you told me that I must not care about the quality of my work. I thought you deserved to know the impact of your words on me.

Keep in mind that now you are dealing with a new issue, not the old one that led you to have the original discussion. Treat this conversation as separate from the original conversation; craft a new ABC message, deliver it at an appropriate time, then be prepared to actively listen.

If the other person reacts in a way that makes you really uncomfortable, remember to shut the duck up because whatever you say when your basic instincts are triggered is only going to make things worse. When you lose control of yourself, you lose influence and power. You don't want this conversation to get sidetracked and become about something stupid that you said. When we react instead of remain calm, it undermines our credibility and detracts from the importance of our message. Feel free to exit tough conversations when you need to and don't worry about your dignity or the integrity of your message. By being transparent about your discomfort and refusing to retaliate out of defensiveness or anger, you convey confidence and add power to your message. You want to be able to walk away from the conversation with your head held high, secure in the knowledge that you did not sink to dirty tactics or let yourself get provoked, that instead you kept cool and focused. Of course, the other reason to exercise all of this self-restraint (including walking away when necessary) is because you want results - and using these tools will make it that much easier to get what you want.

"Nobody can make you feel inferior without your consent."

- Eleanor Roosevelt

Give Yourself a Break: We all Mess Up!

Despite all the good intentions and tools in the world, we all mess up from time to time. There are many times I catch myself ranting and raving and violating every principle I promote. It's not pretty. Then I recover and remember to get over myself because another opportunity to do better is always just around the corner (and often comes sooner than I expect!). The key is how you handle your mistakes, not whether you make them. If you say something unkind or indulge your basic instincts to fight, flee or fold, then stop and apologize for what you said or did without inserting a "but" after your apology (as in, "I am sorry I called you 'delusional,' but you were kind of acting like a crazy person"). This is what I would call a non-apology because it just negates the "I'm sorry" part of your sentence. Comments like this do more damage than saying nothing at all. (We will talk more about apologies in chapter 14.)

Top Tools to Recall: Staying Cool

- ✔ Remind yourself that their reactions are not personal.
- ✔ Observe rather than participate in the drama. Try playing "name that hook!"
- ✔ Adopt a calming, positive mantra for when things heat up.
- ✔ Exit the conversation if you can't take the heat.

Yay! You now know how to be a better communicator than the vast majority of people out there because you have the tools not just to get your message across, but to stay cool even if the other person freaks out big time. Others can try as much as they want to hook you into reacting, but now you know better and will hopefully be able to manage even the toughest of tough conversations. Now get ready to kick your listening skills up a notch; when you do, you'll find it that much more effortless to guide your conversation towards a successful conclusion.

Tame the Elephant in the Office
(in 4 pretty easy steps)

Step 1: Prepare to Talk

Get clear about what the real issue is and write it down in three sentences or less. Then determine what your ultimate goal is for the conversation. Be realistic.

Step 2: Design and Deliver Your "ABC Message"

What do you say and how do you say it? It's as easy as "ABC:" make it Accurate, Brief and Clear. Don't waste your time dancing around the issue; be honest and give people the "straight goods" in a way that is respectful and nonjudgmental.

Step 3: Stop Talking and Start Listening

Once you have delivered your ABC message, listen without interruption to hear the other person out. This may be your toughest challenge, but it is essential to keep the conversation on track... and it is easier than you think!

Step 4: Respond Powerfully

This is your opportunity to respond (not react) and clarify in a way that is confident, concise and clear. No excuses. No justifications. No blame.

Chapter 12:

Tell Me More

Chapter highlights:

- ☐ *When possible, take your listening skills up a notch.*
- ☐ *Ask questions of the "tell me more" variety.*
- ☐ *Acknowledge the other person's perspective and concerns.*

"To listen well is as powerful a means of communication and influence as to talk well."

- John Marshall[26]

Warning: This chapter is not for the faint of heart! Why? Well, at this point if you still want to cut someone down to size with a sarcastic or snide comment, then you are not ready to take your listening skills up to the next level. That's what this chapter is all about – kicking up your listening skills a notch or two. If you can do it, the benefits promise to be phenomenal. If you are not there yet, that's okay – it will come with practice. As you gain confidence in having these difficult conversations, all of this will get easier and may eventually even feel - dare I say it - nearly effortless.

Listening 2.0: Power Tools to Take Your Listening Skills Up a Notch

I am about to share with you some additional tools you can use to really propel your tough conversations in the right direction. If these feel too difficult right now, feel free not to use them just yet. They aren't strictly necessary for a successful conversation, but keep the ideas around for when you *do* have the confidence to give them a shot, because they really can help.

Tool #1: Ask "tell me more" questions.

Picture this: the other person is having a freak-out and you are calm, cool and confident. You may even be curious about what is going on for the other person. At this point, you may want to step back into the conversation and ask some more questions to really get to the bottom of things. Then comes the really tough part: listen to the answers to tease out what is really going on from the other person's perspective. Let's look at some examples now.

If the other person says you are unfair, you might say:

- ✔ I am wondering why you would say that.
- ✔ Tell me more about how you think I am being unfair.

If the other person says that something is all your fault because you are disorganized, you could say:

- ✔ Would you explain why you feel I am disorganized?
- ✔ I am wondering why you think this is my fault.

If the other person accuses you of not trusting him or her, you could ask:

- ✔ I am not sure how trust is related to my asking about XYZ. Would you explain?
- ✔ What does trust mean to you?

If the other person says something like, "You are the one who is disrespectful!" you might respond:

- ✔ I am wondering why you would say that.
- ✔ Please tell me more about what it is I am doing that has led you to feel that way.

If the other person accuses you of being deceitful or misleading, you could ask:

- ✔ What leads you to say that I have deceived/misled you?
- ✔ Would you say more about why you feel that I have deceived/misled you?

If the other person says that you are unreasonable (or that your decision is), you might want to say:

- ✔ Tell me more about your thinking.
- ✔ I am wondering what about this decision seems unreasonable. Could you tell me more?
- ✔ What have I done that you believe is unreasonable?

If you are having trouble coming up with just the right words, try this little phrase (it works like a charm!):

> "I am wondering why you would say that."

It's a simple yet disarming statement. The key is to say it (or any of the other statements/questions) calmly, with confidence and no attitude. Asking good questions can help you get to the heart of what is going on and paves the way to go from feeling triggered to feeling confident. Ask your question and then immediately stop talking and embrace silence. Focus and listen to the other person's responses. You've done this before, so it shouldn't feel too unfamiliar, even though it's coming at a later stage in the conversation.

A note of caution: remember that whenever you speak at this stage, you are taking a big risk. Choose your moments carefully. Can you see how the statements and questions above could be taken the wrong way if you speak with the wrong tone? If there is a hint of insincerity or sarcasm in your voice, it will be picked up by the other person instantly and your conversation will go sideways in a heartbeat, so only do this if you are feeling confident that you can speak in a neutral tone. Take a deep breath and think friendly before you ask questions about the other person's rude, snarky or judgmental remarks.

Tool #2: Acknowledge the other person's perspective and concerns.

Here's another tool that should sound familiar: check out your understanding of what the other person has said, even if the comment is rude, snarky, judgmental or just plain mean. Clarify the other person's take on things so you don't get too off track. Here are some examples:

> After you have asked your "tell me more" question about being unfair and then listened closely to the other person's rationale, you might say:
>
> ✔ It sounds like you don't think this decision is fair and you would like me to change my decision. Is that it?
>
> After you have asked your "tell me more" question about why you were called "disorganized," you listen intently to the explanation and then say something like:
>
> ✔ So, you believe that if I question your ideas in a meeting, then I am undermining your credibility. Is that right?
>
> After you have asked your "tell me more" question about not trusting your employee and you hear her say that you are asking too much, you could respond:
>
> ✔ So, you think that when I asked you to take care of that task, I was asking too much of you. Have I got it right?
>
> After you have asked your "tell me more" question about being called "deceitful," your colleague says that you are a "glory hog." You might want to say:

- ✓ Okay, you feel that I should have ensured your work was given credit. Is that it?
- ✓ I can understand why you would be frustrated. Tell me more about what you had hoped the outcome would be.

Again, if you aren't sure what to say and still aren't clear on the other person's perspective, just keep it simple and say:

"Tell me more."

Why Do These Techniques Work?

By asking questions and really listening to the answers, you are far more likely to get to the heart of the matter and get a better picture of where other people are coming from. What are their perspectives? What are their concerns? Remember, your goal is to listen through their "hot" language in order to learn their stories. Listen like a child listens to a storyteller: with curiosity and no expectation of what might come next. If we take other people's responses at face value, react to snarky comments or use "hot" language of our own, we don't learn anything. We don't know what they are really talking about or where they are really coming from... and that can lead to conversations that just go around and around in circles, with insults and judgments ricocheting everywhere, with no productive ending in sight.

When you get to the bottom of what is really going on, not only are you in a better position of understanding the issue, but you also have accomplished the added bonus of making the other person feel heard. Everyone wants to be understood and taken seriously. When things get strained in conversations, people rarely feel heard and, when we don't feel heard, we also stop listening... and when listening stops, respect flies out the window. Once respect is gone, well, things get out of control - and no good can come of that.

"Setting an example is not the main means of influencing another, it is the only means."

- Albert Einstein

On the other hand, when people feel heard in their difficult conversations, not only do they feel relieved and surprised, but they are also unexpectedly disarmed. They were stockpiling a whole bunch of "hot" language for a fight that never came. Once people are disarmed, their defenses tend to come down, the tension eases and then, as if by magic, they are more likely to listen to your perspective and expectations. When you listen, you dismantle the sense of competition in a conversation. When you don't listen, you add fuel to the fire and people's freak-outs can continue indefinitely (yuck!). Make it easier on everyone by choosing to listen through all of their blustering, rude remarks or other inappropriate behavior. It's the quickest way to find the light at the end of the tunnel and achieve success in your difficult conversations.

As you may have noticed, the skills above are not so much "new" as they are a continuation of skills you've already learned. What makes them extra tricky is that you have to endure the onslaught even longer. There may be more insults, more name-calling, more temper tantrums, more tears. The ball is in your court as far as remaining calm and asking "tell me more" questions for as many rounds as it takes to (a) get the information you need and (b) disarm the other person by listening.

Let's take a look at how we can use our advanced listening skills in some fiery workplace conversations to guide them to a productive conclusion.

Dealing With Disrespectful Behavior: Dragon Dallas

Imagine you are the human resources manager and your director, Dragon Dallas, is known to be practically impossible to work for. Dallas is abrasive, arrogant and apparently fearless. She yells at staff in public, slams doors and stomps around so that most people would never dare to get in her way. You are the human buffer between Dallas and the rest of the staff and are pretty much at the end of your rope dealing with everyone's complaints about her. Avoiding Dallas or your staff is clearly not going to work. You find yourself in an impossible situation because in the past when you have talked to Dallas about these issues, she has informed you that you just don't "get it;" she has checked with the staff herself and there are apparently no problems at all (as if anyone would dare to tell her otherwise!).

During the latest Dragon Dallas drama, Dallas marched into the reception area, which was full of clients, and yelled at the receptionist to get his act together and stop putting calls through to her because she was "too f#!%in' busy." The receptionist was obviously distraught, plus more than a few wide-eyed customers overheard the incident and were understandably horrified.

There is a lot at stake here: this kind of behavior negatively affects relationships within the office and does not leave a good impression with clients. You know you have to talk with Dallas again, but what can you say? Experience tells you that Dallas is going to attack, minimize the incident and be very aggressive. You are ready for whatever she throws your way. You meet with Dallas and deliver your well thought-out ABC message:

> "Dallas, it has come to my attention that on Thursday you came into the reception area and told Martin in a loud voice to get his act together and not put calls through when you were working. I am concerned because Martin felt humiliated and a number of customers and staff have commented to me that they were very uncomfortable with what happened."

You stop talking and, without any hesitation, Dallas predictably responds in a condescending tone, telling you that it really wasn't a big deal. She then barks, "Really, I wish you would stop bothering me with these minor things. I don't have time for this crap! Don't I pay you to take care of this?" You knew this was coming (or some variation on the theme), so you have been chanting your positive, calming, centering mantra. Then, you acknowledge Dallas' perspective:

> "It sounds like you think this is a minor issue and I am overreacting. You want me to deal with these kinds of problems without bothering you. Is that it?"

Dallas yells, "What is wrong with you? Can't you hear? That's what I just said!" You don't take the bait (especially since the hook was accusing you of bad hearing, when you just demonstrated that you have fabulous hearing!). Instead, you take a deep breath, refocus on your goal and respond:

> "I believe this is a bigger issue. You're right; it is my job to handle these things and that is why I am talking to you now. Many employees are intimidated by your behavior. I believe it is negatively affecting morale and our reputation with customers. I am not saying that it is your intention to intimidate or humiliate people. I do believe at times though that that is how your behavior is experienced by others."

Then Dallas tells you she feels that she is being unfairly judged. You ask her to tell you more about that. She goes on for a bit about the company's expectations of her and how hard she works. You pay attention and listen to her. You find out how much pressure she is under, both at work and with a few personal issues on the home front. She is struggling to cope and can't afford to lose her job. You put yourself in her shoes and acknowledge the tremendous amount of stress she must be under. Then you say:

> "Dallas, it sounds like you don't want to intimidate or humiliate people; you just want to get things done. I don't think it is an either/or situation. I am wondering how I can support you to be your best and to soften your approach with our staff. I believe this will go a long way towards improving our bottom line."

This is a good start to what might be a number of conversations that will hopefully make things better for Dallas, the rest of the staff and - oh, right - you, too. Remember that most people don't set out to be difficult and miserable; listening and acknowledging really can work miracles.

Dealing With Rude Behavior: Gutless Gordon

You are the vice president of a public relations firm. You've learned that one of your managers, Gutless Gordon, sent out a negative email about you to the team and even copied the CEO. Uh, hello? What's with this guy anyway? Doesn't he know you're the flippin' VP? You are furious when you find out. You already think Gordon is a worm: insecure, completely gutless and harboring a grudge because you recently got the job he was hoping for (and didn't deserve, by the way). That's the story your inside voice has created and it suits you just fine. However, what are the cold, hard facts? The facts are that Gutless Gordon has indeed sent out an email questioning your leadership, in which he referred to you as "incompetent." The assumptions you are entertaining about *why* he did it may not be the truth because, after all, you don't really know for sure. You just know that you are not happy about it, so you prepare and then deliver your ABC message to Gutless Gordon:

> "Gordon, I am concerned about some recent communication that you sent out. It has come to my attention that you sent an email to the team and the CEO in which you questioned my leadership and referred to me as 'incompetent.' I am not sure what this is all about. Can you tell me what is going on?"

You stop talking, embrace silence and start listening. As you had anticipated, Gutless Gordon responds aggressively by turning the tables on you. He tells you that he is not the only one who is concerned about your leadership and that you shouldn't be picking on him. He thinks you have a lot to learn in your new job and is just trying to be "helpful" (yeah, right). You are tempted to jump in and say something, but fortunately you are prepared so you resist the urge. You feel you still don't have the full picture so you ask a clarifying question like:

> "I wonder if you could tell me more about why you would say I am incompetent and have a lot to learn. Would you elaborate?"

Then you embrace silence again and listen. This question prompts Gordon to reveal the real reason he is upset: He is angry because he recently worked on a very successful project that made the company a lot of money and does not feel he got the credit he deserved. He believes it was your responsibility as VP to ensure that the CEO knew what a great job he had done. Now, you are in no mood to give this weasel any credit whatsoever, but you calm that inside voice and put yourself in his shoes. You acknowledge that if it were you, you would be upset too. So, you agree in a neutral and calm way to make sure his contribution is recognized by everyone, including the CEO.

Gutless Gordon is now disarmed (good job!), but you still have a few issues to clarify. You tell Gordon you are open to feedback when he comes directly to you but sending negative emails will not be tolerated. Of course you have a backup plan (disciplinary action), should this happen again.

Summing Up

Not every conversation is going to be transformative, like the Dragon Dallas talk, or enlightening, like with Gutless Gordon. Not every conversation is even going to have a happy ending. However, as you use the tools you have learned and gain experience and confidence in your difficult conversations, you will be able to improve upon both your skills and your successes. Not every conversation will be tied up neatly with a pretty bow; a series of conversations may be required, sometimes you will need to endure multiple rounds of "tell me more" clarification questions followed by more listening and, often, things won't go exactly according to plan... but you will never get the outcomes you want if you don't get started.

Top Tools to Recall: Advanced Listening Skills

- ✔ Take your listening skills up a notch, but only if you can be sincere in the delivery.
- ✔ Ask "tell me more" questions to clarify.
- ✔ Acknowledge the other person's perspective and concerns to make it more likely that you will be heard and that your conversation will remain respectful.
- ✔ Lead by example; when you create an atmosphere of respect, people are more likely to be disarmed.

You have become a master at embracing silence as well as listening and asking questions to get to the bottom of what is going on for the other person. With this increased awareness comes your best chance to move this conversation forward. I did promise that you would have your opportunity to respond - and here it comes. The trick, of course, is to respond in a way that moves your conversation toward its productive conclusion, rather than send it skidding into the ditch. It *can* be done!

Tame the Elephant in the Office

(in 4 pretty easy steps)

Step 1: Prepare to Talk

Get clear about what the real issue is and write it down in three sentences or less. Then determine what your ultimate goal is for the conversation. Be realistic.

Step 2: Design and Deliver Your "ABC Message"

What do you say and how do you say it? It's as easy as "ABC:" make it Accurate, Brief and Clear. Don't waste your time dancing around the issue; be honest and give people the "straight goods" in a way that is respectful and nonjudgmental.

Step 3: Stop Talking and Start Listening

Once you have delivered your ABC message, listen without interruption to hear the other person out. This may be your toughest challenge, but it is essential to keep the conversation on track... and it is easier than you think!

Step 4: Respond Powerfully

This is your opportunity to respond (not react) and clarify in a way that is confident, concise and clear. No excuses. No justifications. No blame.

Step 4:

Respond Powerfully

Chapter 13: Respond, Don't React

Chapter 14: The Ultimate Power Tool

Chapter 13:

Respond, Don't React

Chapter highlights:

- ☐ *Resist the urge to react and become defensive.*
- ☐ *Educate others about the impact of their behavior without blame or shame.*
- ☐ *Respond powerfully and appropriately to misunderstandings, excuses, inconsistencies, misinformation and statements that you don't agree with.*

You have been pretty patient up to this point, haven't you? In the interest of having a successful conversation, you have given the other person space to digest your message, listened through reactions and asked clarifying questions. You have diligently calmed that know-it-all chatty inside voice and that callous on your lip is proof that you did indeed shut the duck up. You prepared, anticipated and exercised serious self-control. I know that's a lot of work - and now you may be saying to yourself, "Yeah, but what about *me*?"

Now, as promised, it is finally your turn to respond. All of your active listening up to this point is very important because it not only helps you figure out what to say, but it also sets the stage for the other person to actually hear your response. There are two

> "Maintaining an authentic presence is the single most important thing you can do to increase your effectiveness when working to turn conflict into collaboration."
>
> – James W. Tamm[27]

things to keep in mind as you go forward here: First, remember that brief is still best; even if you feel you have lots to say, do everyone a favor and pare down your message to the bare essentials. Just because you have managed to pay attention for what felt like a century doesn't mean that you can expect the same superstar listening skills from the other person. Keep it brief. Second, make sure that the other person is actually done talking as opposed to jumping in when you feel that "enough is enough, already!" Listen all the way through what the other person needs to say; then you'll know that it truly is your turn to respond.

Resist the Urge to Respond Defensively

Although you have managed to embrace silence long enough for the other person to finish talking, you may be tempted to react defensively when it is your turn to respond, even though you know better. Defensiveness can be like a tornado whirling up inside of you while you listen; it's a very natural instinct that is unfortunately not very helpful in your difficult conversations.

Here are some ways that we sometimes disguise our defensive reactions as legitimate responses:

- ✗ I'm right and you're wrong!
- ✗ Perhaps you didn't get it; let me try again to explain it to you - and here are some extra facts/figures/charts/graphs/research/reports/studies...
- ✗ That is just not true! I am not that kind of person.
- ✗ Look, this is not my fault.

Remember how it felt when the other person was being defensive? You didn't believe a word of it. Well, it's the same story here. All you are doing with defensiveness is prolonging the conversation and frittering your power away. Responding defensively reignites the fire you worked so hard to put out because it elicits more reactions and defensiveness in the other person. The more you protest, the more questionable your intentions and motives become. You have worked very diligently to get to this point in your conversations, so ask yourself if you really want to risk undermining your credibility now, when you have come so far. Although defensiveness can be very alluring, it is never the answer.

Let's dig a little deeper into the defensive responses from above and see why they really must be avoided:

1. *"I'm right, you're wrong, so let me show you the light!"*

You want to be careful that your response does not try to convince the other person that your decision, perspective or feelings are "right." Your ABC message may have been brilliant, but forcing people to agree with you so you can make them "see the light" is a fantasy. Maybe they really didn't get it the first time, but there is no chance that they will get it this time, either, if you adopt the quintessentially defensive "I'm right, you're wrong" approach. No matter how hard you try, your attempt to shove your position or perspective down their unwilling throats is doomed to fail.

Think back to the story of Dragon Dallas in the previous chapter. What if the office manager had tried to convinced Dallas that she was "just plain difficult" instead of seeking to understand her? What if she had raised her voice over Dallas' (no easy feat!) and shouted, "Look, lady, do you want to poll the waiting room right now? Everyone thinks you're horrible!" What if she had casually left a copy of the book *Working With You Is Killing Me* on her desk?[28] How convinced would Dallas have been that she was indeed a "dragon?" More importantly, how likely would it have been that Dallas would change her ways? Not very!

My advice is to stop pushing your views on other people because it simply will not get you what you want. People hate to lose face or be told they are wrong. The goal of your talk was never to prove that you were right, anyway (at least I hope not). After all, "rightness" is a pretty subjective concept. Sure, it feels good to be "right," but it will feel even better when you know that you sidestepped that defensive urge in order to achieve your real goals for the conversation. Remember that "being right" is not necessary for you to achieve your goals, so there is no point in trying to force the other person to see things your way.

2. *"You just don't get it. Let me explain again."*

Another defensive approach we adopt is to justify or rationalize our points of view by correcting other people's interpretations of them and then blabbing on and on to explain the "why" of our actions, comments and decisions in painful detail. Just don't go there, no matter how strong the temptation. They won't hear a word of your explanation, I can promise you that, because they will be too busy feeling attacked or patronized. I'm not saying that you shouldn't clarify what you genuinely believe to be a misunderstanding, but don't kid yourself into thinking that if other people don't share your point of view, it must be because they "just don't get it." It is entirely possible for people to maintain two opposing points of view, but that doesn't stop you from sharing your perspective. There is no need to convince people that your stance is more valid than theirs, so don't waste your breath with lengthy justifications and rationalizations. When there is truly something that needs to be clarified, choose a neutral tone of voice and just get to the point.

Here is a little work scenario that many of us can relate to: You work in the accounting department and are completely sick of "urgent requests." You have told one of the worst offenders, Pushy Patrick, that you will not violate policy and write him a check without the proper paperwork. He responds by begging, flattering and trying to convince you to do otherwise.

Does Patrick not understand the policy? Of course he does; he just doesn't like it. Instead of being calm and confident, you defend your decision by explaining in excruciating bureaucratic detail the company's policies and why you are ethically and morally bound to comply. Not only is your speech irritating, but it also gives Patrick plenty of extra semantics to argue with you, which guarantees a lengthy, tedious conversation.

Instead, you could have simply taken a deep breath and said:

> "I understand that you don't agree with this policy and you think it is unfair. You need to know that I am not comfortable violating the rules and I will not be issuing the check without the required paperwork. If you bring me the proper paperwork, I will be happy to write that check for you." STOP TALKING. (Enough said.)

As you can see, it makes much more sense (and is far less painful) to just get to the point and avoid defending yourself by justifying your choices. You can certainly explain the "why" of your decisions to people, but don't bend over backwards rationalizing if they refuse to agree with your explanation. Remember: others do not have to agree with your "why" in order for your conversations to get where they need to go.

3. "That's not true! You know I'm not that kind of person!"

Almost everyone's knee-jerk response is to defend themselves when someone calls into question their character or integrity. While it is tempting to indulge this defensive reaction, remember that this kind of response is unproductive and unlikely to change the other person's perspective. The more you repeat that you are trustworthy, fair, honest, professional, etc., the less convincing it sounds. Besides, there is a good chance that the other person didn't even mean exactly what he or she said, but just blurted it out thanks to defensiveness and a chattering inside voice. You know what that's like, right? There is no point in indulging those judgmental comments with a defensive reaction because it will only serve to send your discussion off in an unwelcome direction.

Let's see if you can relate to this story of denial: Imagine that you are a manager and have just advised Connie that she will not be going to an upcoming national meeting being held in an exotic location and that Fred will be going instead. Connie protests because there are specific presentations related to her work that she thinks she should be a part of, but your answer is a firm "no." Next, a pouting Connie says, "Well, everyone knows that Fred is your favorite, so I guess it's no big surprise that he gets to go and not me!" Now you feel triggered because your integrity has just been called into question. You defend yourself by explaining that it just so happens that Fred has never had the opportunity to go to one of these meetings and that each member of the team should get to have the experience. You natter on and on, telling Connie that you are always as fair as possible, that you do your best to treat everyone the same and that Fred is not your "favorite" because you don't have "favorites." Your conversation, which had originally been about telling Connie she was not going to this meeting, has now gone completely off track and is somehow all about you and your integrity. Your feelings are hurt; Connie is fuming. By responding defensively, all you did was undermine your credibility and fuel Connie's outrage.

So what could you have done instead? First, you could have listened to Connie and acknowledged her perspective like this:

> "It sounds like you really think that you should go to the meeting because the presentations link specifically to your work. I can understand why you would want to be a part of these presentations. It sounds like you are concerned that I am not being fair. Is that right?"
> STOP TALKING and listen.

Once Connie had said what she needed to say, you could have responded in a way that was concise, calm and confident:

> "I understand that you don't think my decision to take Fred to the meeting is fair. I have a different perspective. I believe it is important for all members of the team to experience these meetings even if they are not the lead on the file, so this time Fred will be going."

End of story. Don't worry about defending yourself against Connie's unkind words; dispelling her accusations is unnecessary to get your point across because they do not change the goal for your conversation.

4. *"Hey, I wish things could be different, too, but this really isn't my fault."*

When you don't take ownership of your actions or decisions, ultimately it makes you look weak and ineffectual. Telling people that a workplace decision was out of your control may make you feel better, but ask yourself this: Do *you* respect someone who blames others?

Let's say that you are a human resources manager in a large organization. Recently, a big shakeup decision was made that all of your staff will need to relocate from their field offices to one centralized location. Your employees will all either have to move or find another job. You have worked with some of these people for years; this is really tough for you. You let your employees know and they are all understandably upset and stressed out by the decision. You feel terrible about what is happening and really don't want to be seen as "the bad guy," so you remind your staff that this decision came from head office and that if you could have stopped it, you would have.

How do your employees respond? Well, instead of saying, "Oh, it's okay, this isn't your fault. We'll all be fine," like you had hoped, they continue to grumble and worry - and now you are starting to get the silent treatment.

The reason that everyone is giving you the cold shoulder is because you have made the issue about your fear of being blamed instead of being empathetic about what your employees are going through. When you deflect blame - even if something really isn't your fault - it just makes people upset.

How could you have responded instead? How about:

> "I know this is not an easy time for anyone and you have some difficult decisions ahead of you. I will support you in whatever way I can."

Much better! This statement is more likely to give the staff a sense of calm and support. By not diverting your conversation down the "this isn't my fault" path, you keep focused on the issue and show that you respect what others are going through.

So you see the problems defensiveness can cause, but now you may be asking, "What about setting the record straight? Can't I have the satisfaction of pointing out people's flawed arguments? Or what if I'm really not to blame?" The problem with "setting the record straight" is that it tells the other person that you feel the need to bolster your message. It ultimately shows a lack of confidence, which undermines your credibility and power. Lengthy explanations, justifying, denying and blaming just give the other person more material to disagree with and argue about. Worst of all, your initial message gets lost in the shuffle because you have lost focus of your goal.

Down With Defensiveness: Fabulous Fridays

Let me tell you a story from my personal life that showcases how defensiveness can get in the way:

I enjoy Friday as a day to do lots of creative work in my home office. No one else is in the house: no kids, no housekeeper, no hubby. Periodically, though, hubby takes Fridays off. He'll use his day to get caught up in his home office, exercise, take the kids to school, do errands, etc. His intentions are always good. He wants to be helpful and supportive - but the reality for me is that when he is home, I don't get much done. One such week, hubby told me cheerfully he had the coming Friday off and asked what he could do to help out. He also wanted to know if I would like to go to the gym with him and then go for lunch, then maybe fit in a tennis game. I put on a weak smile and said, "Let's see how the week unfolds."

The next morning, I offhandedly mentioned to my son that I was a little disappointed that dad's Friday off kind of messed with my plans. Well, not only was this not a nice thing to say, especially to my son, but later that evening when we all sat down to dinner, my son announced, "Dad, you should go to work on Friday. Mom said she doesn't want you around the house because you are always messing up her plans." Hubby stopped mid-chew and looked at me with a mix of disappointment and hurt. And what did I do? I did what many of us do when we get caught with our pants down: panic!

First, I employed the classic defensive maneuver of denial. I denied making the statement, but my son would have none of that - he knew what he'd heard! Next, I denied saying it the way my son had portrayed me saying it. I lamely said something along the lines of, "No, I didn't say that. What I said was that it can be difficult to get work done when anyone is home; it's nothing personal." Well, my son busted me on that one as well and informed the table that that was *not* what I had said (ah, from the mouths of babes). So then I tried justifying my comments, adding in a little bit of blame for good measure: "Well, the problem is that when you're home, you don't respect that I'm working. You talk too loudly on the phone. You expect me to chat and want to go to the gym together, play tennis and have lunch. I also have to clean up after your messes. It's actually *more* work for me!"

Needless to say, this conversation was not going very well. I had undermined my message with denial and story-changing, not to mention I had set a bad example for my son and hurt hubby's feelings. He had been excited about spending the day at home, hoping to have some quality time with his wife and kids. Sheesh - nicely done, Diane!

If I had a "do-over," there are a number of things I would have done differently: First, I would have kept my inside voice at bay and not have made that comment in front of my son. Second, I would have owned up to what I'd said and apologized instead of getting defensive and turning the tables on my son and hubby. Finally, I would have found an opportunity to chat with my hubby (in private, away from the kids) to clarify why I had made the comment in the first place. The idea would be not to give up on what I wanted, which was time on my Fridays to go about my day, but to share my concerns with my husband so that we could work something out together.

I could have said something like:

"Honey, I wanted to let you know where I was coming from when I made that comment. I was looking forward to getting a lot of work done on Friday as my week is pretty booked up. It wasn't my intention to give you the impression that I don't like having you around or appreciate your help - because I really do. I'm wondering how we could schedule these kinds of days going forward so we both can get our needs met."

Learning to Respond Powerfully

What we *really* want to do is respond powerfully... but when we get defensive, we fall short of our intentions. Since you can't change what you don't know, being aware of what makes you feel defensive can help you manage those feelings rather than fall victim to them. Our triggers are often comments that call into question our fairness, integrity, competence, honesty, commitment or trustworthiness. Remember to try a little positive mantra when you are up to the plate and it is time to respond. Choose to respond powerfully, not defensively. Be concise, calm and confident. That's the best way to get your message heard.

As communicators, we are powerful when we are influential, effective and persuasive. This is especially true in our most difficult conversations, when we are tasked with responding powerfully in the face of an intimidating reaction. If you are naturally shy or timid, facing a freak-out can seem terrifying. How are you supposed to stand up to all of that shouting and/or crying and/or intimidation? Just remember the tools you have learned throughout this book. Zero in on your goal and remain focused throughout the talk. Pluck up the courage to speak and don't worry about the other person's defensive reactions - no matter how off-the-wall - because now you know that all you have to do is embrace silence (not too hard for someone who is afraid to speak!) and listen closely until it is your turn to respond and reiterate your message.

On the flip side, for those of you who tend to be more "bull in a china shop" than "wallflower," know that I have learned the hard way that "responding powerfully" is not the same as "overpowering people." Coming across as abrasive or dominating is not a smart tack for successful conversations.

"Being powerful is like being a lady. If you have to tell people you are, you aren't."
- Margaret Thatcher

A number of years ago, I took a communications course. I thought I was doing an especially terrific job in the difficult conversation role-plays. On the final day, my instructor gave me some very candid feedback on a videotaped conversation role-play. She described my eye contact as laser-like and my presence and tone as overpowering. She said my physical proximity to the other person while I was talking made me intimidating. I was surprised by the feedback because I was apparently saying all the "right words," but my voice and body language told a different story. The instructor told me that I needed to work on my empathy (putting myself in the other person's shoes) and soften my approach.

Afterward, I was chatting with one of my classmates about the feedback, assuming he would protest and tell me how brilliant I really was. Instead, he sort of laughed and said, "You know, Diane, as soon as you walked in the room on the first day of the course, I decided I was going to avoid you like the plague. Even though you did not tell us you were a lawyer initially, it oozed out of every pore of your body. I felt really sorry for your husband. I was totally afraid of you! I am glad I got to know you better because now I realize you are a great lady."

Wow! I was surprised! That day, I learned that body language is so potent that it can send a message well before you ever get the chance to open your mouth during what you think is supposed to be your shot to make a first impression. I was grateful that my classmate had allowed himself to get to know me; but who knows how many others in my life just decided to stay away?

When we can be more approachable and less "in your face," it gives us the opportunity to create more powerful messages. Remember that "power" is about being heard and sharing your message, not about dominating others. It is about being true to yourself and what you believe in, without discounting other people or their perspectives. You want to respond in a way that is calm, concise and confident with the big picture in mind.

And How Am I Supposed to Do *That*?

It *is* possible to educate others about the impact of their behavior without blame or shame - and without cowering while we do it. We can still hold people accountable by exposing assumptions, biases or misinformation. Share your observation or opinion; just do it without the "hot" and judgmental language that you know would put your conversation in jeopardy. Let's look at how you can respond powerfully in a few sample situations now:

1. *Responding powerfully to misunderstandings*

If it becomes obvious that there have been misunderstandings in your talk, don't be afraid to clarify your message or ask further questions to ensure that you understand each other. It may take a few rounds of clarifying questions and genuine listening, but the effort will pay off. Keep in mind that you don't necessarily want to take everything the person says at face value because chances are you might be speaking to a defensive inside voice. Dig a little deeper and do your best to clarify without condescension.

Instead of this:

- ✗ I guess you misunderstood me. Let me explain it *again*. [You might as well have said, "You are obviously too stupid to have gotten it the first time!"]

- ✗ You must not be listening; let's try again. [Sounds like blame to me!]

- ✗ If you had been paying attention at all, you would know that that isn't what I said. [Yikes - just yikes.]

Say this:

- ✔ It sounds like I have not explained myself very well. Could I clarify?
- ✔ It certainly was not my intention to imply that you are incompetent. My concern is...
- ✔ I must not have expressed myself well; I don't want there to be any misunderstandings. I would like to clarify that...

2. *Responding powerfully to long-winded defensive flare-ups*

Sometimes, after the other person has responded defensively and gone on and on and on, you may sense that your message fell overboard at some point. For the sake of keeping your talk on track, be sure to calmly and clearly restate your message. Avoid cutting the other person off (no matter how tempting), but once it is your turn to speak, try to get the conversation back on track.

Instead of this:

- ✗ I *am* being fair and my decision is final!
- ✗ Look, it's rude to be texting nonstop and checking your emails at a lunch meeting, period.

Say this:

- ✔ It sounds like you don't think I am being fair here and that I am singling you out. I have a different perspective.
- ✔ My expectation is that we are all fully engaged at meetings and, for me, that means no texting or checking email.

3. *Responding powerfully to lame excuses*

Other people often don't take responsibility for their actions, happily offering up a litany of excuses for why they haven't done what they should have. You obviously don't buy their rationale, but if you attempt to address every last lame excuse, you practically guarantee that more defensiveness is on its way and that your conversation goes from "difficult" to "never-ending."

Instead of this:

✗ I am so sick of all of your excuses!

Say this:

✓ I understand that things come up from time to time. I also need to know that I can count on you to do what you tell me you will do. If there is a problem, I need to know right away so that we can deal with it.

4. *Responding powerfully to inconsistent statements or misinformation*

We have all been in conversations in which one party gets caught in an untruth and then starts backpedaling like crazy. (Just think of me in my "Fabulous Fridays" story; I would have backpedaled all the way to China if I could have!) When you catch people in a lie, it is soooo tempting to nail them to the wall; but when you back people into a corner, you can usually count on them coming out swinging. Honestly, didn't you postpone this difficult conversation for as long as you could just because you wanted to avoid the drama? Don't give in now! Yes, you *can* let people know that you are aware of their inconsistencies and the impact that they have had on you, but that's where it ends. Remember, the goal is not to assume the worst of people or ill intentions on their parts; the goal is to communicate your awareness of the inconsistency and then move on.

Instead of this:

- ✗ That is *not* what you said. You said you didn't talk to the client, but that is obviously not true. Maybe you should get your story straight before you start calling me names!
- ✗ Wow, first it's A, then it's B! Can you even tell the truth from a lie anymore?

Say this:

- ✓ I thought you said that you hadn't talked with the client in advance of our meeting. Now you tell me that, to make the meeting more efficient, you had to come up with a plan with the client.
- ✓ What you deserve to know is that I am concerned that you are changing your story because the issue is now about trust, which is a bigger concern for me.

5. *Responding powerfully to statements that you disagree with*

Often in our difficult conversations, people will say things that we just plain disagree with. We know that we must acknowledge their perspectives but we don't want to come across as agreeing with what has been said. Through your responses, you can choose to either lead your conversation to its productive conclusion or send it into a skid.

Instead of this:

- ✗ I disagree.
- ✗ You are flat-out wrong.

Say this:

- ✓ I have a different perspective.
- ✓ Nothing we have talked about here has changed my view.

Then follow up with clarification of your perspective, such as:

- ✓ It may not have been your intention to shut down communication, but I believe that that was the impact when you rolled your eyes and sighed at Oscar in the meeting this morning.

Hopefully you can see how powerful responses differ from defensive responses. When you choose to respond powerfully, it can make your conversations go much better. Of course, when I say "much better," I don't necessarily mean that the other person is going to be thrilled with your news or that you will get what you want and everyone will live happily ever after. What I do mean is that when you deliver your message with clarity and then respond powerfully in a way that is calm, concise and confident, you make reaching your ultimate goal for the conversation that much easier.

Wrap It Up!

Now that you have responded powerfully and clarified any misunderstandings, it is time to wrap the conversation up. "Wrapping it up" can mean different things depending on how the conversation goes. It really depends on the nature of the conversation in question.

Here are some ways you may want to wrap it up:

- ✔ I have made my position clear. How you decide to handle this is up to you.
- ✔ Let's summarize what we have both understood, here...
- ✔ We have talked about many things today. I would like you to think over your options and get back to me by the end of next week.
- ✔ Just to clarify what we have both understood: you will let me know if you will have trouble meeting your deadlines before the actual due dates.
- ✔ Let's follow up with this matter in three days' time.

If you can, spend a little time thinking about what an appropriate "wrap it up" dialogue might look like for your particular situation before your difficult conversation begins. As you can see, every scenario is different. Choose what might work for your situation, as well as what would feel natural for you to say, then go from there. The "wrap it up" portion of your conversation may not go exactly according to plan, but by anticipating how things might go, you help ensure that you won't get caught without the right words.

Although your message may be a bitter pill to swallow, it *can* be delivered in such a way that the person you are talking to feels heard, feels respected and has the opportunity to save face - just like my friend Scottie did with me. Keep in mind that the choice to save face and respond less defensively is entirely theirs, just as the choice to react defensively or respond powerfully is entirely yours. I obviously can't guarantee that the people in your conversations will disarm, calm down and help you end the conversation maturely and calmly, even when you apply every tool in this book to perfection. I can't promise that you will never be interrupted, that there will never be tears or that your conversations will always be as smooth as silk.

"The real art of conversation is not only to say the right thing in the right place, but... to leave unsaid the wrong thing at the tempting moment."

- Dorothy Nevill[29]

What I can promise is that when you stick to these tools, you will be able to leave difficult workplace conversations knowing that you did everything in your power to ensure they go as well as possible and that you took the high road, even when the other person's defensive reactions and freak-outs were taunting you mercilessly. You will have conveyed your message confidently, listened respectfully and responded powerfully - and that's all you can ask of yourself. The rest is up to the other person.

Also keep in mind that when we have these kinds of interactions, the results we are hoping for are seldom instantaneous. More often than not, it takes time and space for other people to calm down and think about our perspectives on the matter at hand. It could take hours, days, weeks or longer, and you will probably never hear the other person say those magic words: "You know, you were right!" However, in all likelihood, you *will* start to see a change in the other person's behavior. It isn't 100% guaranteed, of course, and that is what your backup plan is for, but in my experience, a well-executed conversation is often the catalyst for positive and lasting change.

Top Tools to Recall: Responding Powerfully

- ✔ Choose not to react to the other person. Remember to "shut the duck up" when necessary!
- ✔ Help the other person save face by responding powerfully, not defending or trying to prove the other person wrong.
- ✔ Responding powerfully gives you a feeling of control and the confidence of knowing you can be proud of your behavior.
- ✔ Choose to be calm, concise and confident. The rest is up to the other person.

Congratulations! You now have all of the tools you need in order to prepare for your toughest of tough talks and navigate them to a successful outcome... but there is still one trick left that can make all of your difficult conversations go that much easier: a positive relationship.

When you have a good working relationship with another person, it can make having these conversations easier because the mutual respect is already there. I don't mean that the two of you have to be besties, but it does help if the relationship is generally positive. The good news is that (a) you can have your tough talks either way - good relationship or not - and (b) it *is* possible to foster positive relationships in the workplace, even with people whom you don't particularly care for. Get ready to learn some powerful relationship-building tools that can transform you from "great communicator" into "communicator extraordinaire."

SHUT THE DUCK UP!

Tame the Elephant in the Office

(in 4 pretty easy steps)

Step 1: Prepare to Talk

Get clear about what the real issue is and write it down in three sentences or less. Then determine what your ultimate goal is for the conversation. Be realistic.

Step 2: Design and Deliver Your "ABC Message"

What do you say and how do you say it? It's as easy as "ABC:" make it Accurate, Brief and Clear. Don't waste your time dancing around the issue; be honest and give people the "straight goods" in a way that is respectful and nonjudgmental.

Step 3: Stop Talking and Start Listening

Once you have delivered your ABC message, listen without interruption to hear the other person out. This may be your toughest challenge, but it is essential to keep the conversation on track... and it is easier than you think!

Step 4: Respond Powerfully

This is your opportunity to respond (not react) and clarify in a way that is confident, concise and clear. No excuses. No justifications. No blame.

Chapter 14:

The Ultimate Power Tool

Chapter highlights:

- ☐ *Adopt the 5:1 rule.*
- ☐ *Learn to genuinely appreciate your coworkers and colleagues.*
- ☐ *Master the art of saying "I'm sorry."*

The one thing that can make our difficult conversations a whole lot easier is having a solid relationship with the person with whom we need to talk. Whether in our professional or personal lives, when things are humming along, we don't seem to do much talking - but there's no need to wait until we have some humungous catastrophe on our hands to open up the lines of communication.

A proactive approach is often much more productive (and far less threatening to the relationship) than going in after something bad has happened and attempting to put the pieces back together. You can be proactive and foster positive workplace relationships by being transparent about your good feelings, praise, compliments, etc.

We have spent most of the book covering difficult conversations, which in practice often means "negative conversations," such as:

- ✔ Delivering sensitive news
- ✔ Delivering bad or sad news
- ✔ Confronting someone's rudeness or disrespectful behavior
- ✔ Dealing with poor performance
- ✔ Saying "no" to someone who really wants a "yes"

But not all of your important conversations have to be negative. Everyone likes to hear that they have done something well, myself included (and I'm guessing you, too!). Let's end things on a positive note by talking about how to build strong workplace relationships to create a healthier, longer-term big picture, which will ultimately help smooth out any future tough talks.

Adopt the 5:1 Rule

According to renowned relationship expert John Gottman, the "magic ratio" of positive to negative interactions for happily married couples, especially during times of conflict, is 5:1.[30] There was also a study published in *American Behavioral Scientist* that focused on a similar ratio, only in the workplace.[31] That study found that high performing teams had a ratio of positive to negative interactions at work of 5.6:1. In other words, the two findings were similar: five-ish positive interactions for every one negative interaction seems to be the recipe for harmony, both at work and at home.[32]

Honestly, how many of us can say that we are following the 5:1 rule in the workplace? Doesn't it seem like we spend the majority of our time complaining about what people are doing wrong? Instead, let's consciously look for opportunities to "catch" people doing something right and then tell them about it.

Your five positive actions can manifest in a lot of different ways: simple things like being humble or more difficult things like apologizing even when we don't want to. We might seek opportunities to do small favors, such as picking up our coworker's coffee along with our own or helping our peers set up their presentation materials. It all can help improve our workplace relationships and hopefully make our more difficult relationships that much easier. This is not about giving fake compliments to anyone who will listen or showing off how magnanimous you are; it's about a sincere effort to improve the relationships in your workplace through simple, thoughtful words and actions.

Being Genuine Is Key

Never lose sight of this: whatever you do in an effort to improve your relationships must be genuine and come from the heart. If you set out to build your relationships in a way that is mechanical and contrived, people will see through that and your actions may be viewed as manipulative. People can spot insincerity from a mile away.

"Kindness is in our power even when fondness is not."

- Samuel Johnson

If your acts of kindness are aimed at people with whom you already have good working relationships, that's fine. But if your relationship with your colleague, business partner or assistant is strained, then be prepared for some puzzled looks or push-back as you focus on the positive with them and act in genuinely kind ways. Hold your ground and choose not to be defensive if they question your motives. For example, if you say to your assistant, "I really appreciate that you come in early every day to get a head start on your work," she may be suspicious of your intentions and give you a look or say something along the lines of: "I have been coming in early for 10 years and today is no different."

The temptation is to respond, "I was only trying to be nice! Sheesh - can't you take a compliment? Why do you have to be so defensive?" Oops - so much for your niceness. Instead, shut the duck up or you will undo all of your good intentions and set yourself up for a steep uphill battle in the future. We know what happens when we become defensive: it invariably gets us the opposite of what we want. Just embrace silence, smile at the fact that your niceness caught someone by surprise and move on.

When I teach workshops and we talk about the 5:1 rule, I absolutely cringe when managers spend their break time immediately acknowledging or thanking staff members for their hard work. Although well intentioned, it comes across as insincere because it's not specific enough and it's out of context - kind of like when you complain to your beau about how he never buys you flowers and then the next day he shows up with a great big bouquet. Not very impressive. The key is to look for real and timely opportunities to have these positive interactions. If people think you are only doing it because you learned it in a workshop or because you want something from them, they will feel manipulated. Choose an appropriate time and always remember that if you can't be genuine, just don't bother.

Simple Tools for Relationship Building

There are a few important and (mostly) painless tools you can employ to start filling up your relationship bank accounts and working towards the 5:1 ratio:

Tool #1: Show appreciation.

What is "appreciation," anyway? Well, here are some synonyms: gratitude, recognition, a favorable judgment, admiration, respect, acknowledgment. Tell people what you appreciate about them and their work. You'll need to be specific and absolutely genuine, otherwise your efforts will be meaningless at best and seen as a manipulative ploy at worst - neither of which will help to fill up your relationship bank account.

Instead of this:

✗ You do great work. [Too vague.]

Say this:

✓ When you took the time to explain the process to those clients, it really put them at ease. You are a terrific communicator and are very client-focused. Thank you.

Do not think appreciation applies only to your staff or colleagues. Nothing could be further from the truth! I don't know of a boss who couldn't use a little appreciation. I have friends who are

"The deepest principle in human nature is the craving to be appreciated."
- William James[33]

CEOs and VPs and they often tell me how rarely they hear words of appreciation from their teams. Our assumption is that people who hold these esteemed positions must already know they are smart, capable, funny, etc. so they probably don't need to hear it from us. This is generally not at all true; we all have a very basic need to know we are appreciated, that we are doing a good job and that we are well liked.

My advice: give your boss, your troublesome coworker or your assistant some appreciation, even if the relationship is strained. You might be surprised at how far a little kindness can go. And don't forget the people you are closest to! Sometimes we just assume they know how much we appreciate them, so we don't think to tell them so. A close friend of mine is a surgeon and every year he personally bakes an amazing carrot cake for his assistant on her birthday. It is an incredibly thoughtful thing to do and is one way to let his assistant know how much he values all she does for him. Expressing your appreciation does not have to cost a thing and, when genuinely given, can mean a world of difference to the other person. When we can sincerely appreciate the people we work with, it validates what they do on the job and paves the way for smoother communication down the road, if and when difficult situations arise.

Appreciation Emergency: Sid the Star

I was teaching a workshop in which I had a frustrated human resources manager confide in me that she was concerned her organization was about to lose one of its star employees, Sid. It all boiled down to a stereotypical boss who did not show Sid the Star any appreciation or gratitude. All Sid wanted was some acknowledgement for her hard work and appreciation for going the extra mile for this tough boss, who had a reputation for going through employees like underwear.

The frustrated HR manager had tried to tell the boss what she thought was needed, but he just didn't get it. He had said to her, "Sid knows that she is doing a good job. I don't need to tell her! What am I, her mommy?" If only this boss had understood that a few genuine words of appreciation for all of Sid the Star's hard work and dedication could have changed how this employee felt about her job, it may have ensured that Sid remained "Sid the Star" and not "Sid, the employee who quit caring because no one noticed how hard she worked" or "Sid, our former employee who got scooped up by a company who valued her more." How could the boss have done this?

Instead of this:

> ✗ Sid, I just wanted to acknowledge you and your work. [Blah - this is not specific enough and sounds insincere.]

Say this:

> ✓ Sid, I just wanted to let you know how much I appreciated you changing your plans this weekend to take care of the

> Jones project. You did a great job on the report and saved my butt with this important client. Thank you.

Remember that being specific with your praise is better because it helps prove that your comments and intentions are genuine.

Helpful Hint: The Right Time for Appreciation

How do you know when someone really needs to hear some genuine appreciation? A good rule of thumb is that if you find yourself singing someone's praises to other people, make sure you *also* tell the person who really deserves to hear it most.

So, this is all well and good, but isn't it a little hard to imagine being this complimentary and appreciative if we have a troubled relationship with someone? Yes, but it isn't impossible. It just takes some courage and probably a little bit of pride-swallowing. Despite how difficult our relationships have become, if we really focus on what we like in other people and what they contribute to the workplace, we will surely find positive things. Then, once we have found those things, all we have to do is let them know.

One great way to build a bridge in your more strained workplace relationships is to "catch" people doing things right (versus waiting in the shadows for them to screw up). When I was working as a lawyer, I had a poor relationship with my secretary (you know, the one who called me "disorganized" and whom I accused of wasting my time - big shocker that we didn't get along, I know). Most of my interactions with her revolved around me telling her what she had done wrong and how she should change. Not surprisingly, she became increasingly defensive and argumentative, accusing me of interfering with her ability to get things done. It really wasn't working out well for either of us.

Eventually, out of desperation, I decided to try a different tack and made a commitment to myself to try to "catch" her doing something well and then let her know about it. The result was nothing short of amazing. She started to soften her attitude toward me and was more willing to do the work I gave her. When I started to focus on the positive, so did my secretary. When I had focused on the negative before, she did too. By focusing on what is good and working in your relationships instead of what is wrong and not working, you may actually be able to make some of your negative issues disappear. Then not only do you both get what you want in the short term, but when you do end up needing to have a tough conversation down the road (which you inevitably will), it should be a whole lot easier.

If you have a strained work relationship, don't try to pretend that your tough conversation or unfortunate altercation never took place; the longer you do that, the worse things will get. Instead, think about how you can build a bridge so that you can have a friendly - or at least civil - working relationship. You are probably interacting with this person often, so why not do what you can to make your future interactions more pleasant and productive?

Tool #2: Be humble.

Humility can mean a lot of things, including thinking modestly about our accomplishments, a willingness to expose the less-than-perfect parts of ourselves, a readiness to learn from others and perhaps having a laugh or two at our own expense. Humility can strengthen our relationships by keeping our defenses down and paving the way for more productive interactions. Please note that I'm not talking about using fake humility to fish for compliments - I have been guilty of this kind of behavior and believe me, it isn't a relationship-builder. We want to be humble in a positive way; when we can express our vulnerability, that is very powerful. It has a profound impact on how others interact with us. Humility humanizes us, underscores our credibility and opens the lines of communication.

"Swallow your pride occasionally - it's non-fattening!

- Frank Tyger[34]

My hubby, bless his soul, has been a testing ground for much of my work. He has been a good sport and has tried out some of my theories both at work and at home. Hubby is a surgeon and has a large and busy practice with a lot of support staff. He found that, ordinarily, when he sought feedback from his team on how he could improve his management style, he always received very little constructive feedback. At first, he took this to mean that everything must be going swimmingly. I encouraged him to look a little deeper. So, he tried an experiment:

He called an office meeting and asked everyone to complete the following sentence: "You irritate me when you..." Then, he encouraged his staff to itemize all of the things my hubby did that irritated them. It took some prodding and encouragement at first, but as the meeting went on, people became more open and honest about what was going on for them. It turned out to be a very effective team-building strategy because hubby refrained from leaping to his own defense when people shared their frustrations. Instead, he asked "tell me more" questions such as:

> "I didn't realize that. Would you please explain a little further?"

He listened. He clarified their concerns. He acknowledged what they had said and how they felt. I'm sure you can imagine that this wasn't easy to do, especially when the feedback got a little personal. However, hubby swallowed his pride and chose to shut the duck up. And what was the result? He made some changes, but more importantly he sent the message to his staff that he cared about them and was open to hearing their thoughts. Had hubby become defensive, however, the exercise would have backfired and actually made withdrawals from the relationship bank account because he would have shown that he wasn't genuine in being humble and hearing his staff's concerns. If you can manage to be humble and remain genuine while listening to other people, you'll build trust in your relationships big time. (I could not be prouder of that man!)

Tool #3: Apologize when you need to.

Admit it: most of us are really terrible at apologizing. It makes us uncomfortable and somehow we believe deep down that if we apologize, we are undermining our credibility. (If I am not describing you right now, give yourself a big pat on the back because being able to apologize properly is no small feat!) Nothing could be further from the truth: a genuine apology can go a long way in enhancing workplace relationships and your credibility, too.

"Nobody stands taller than those willing to stand corrected."

- William Safire[35]

An apology is much more than uttering, "I'm sorry," especially when your tone and body language suggest otherwise. If you remember nothing else, remember that a half-baked apology does more harm than no apology at all. If you do decide that you need to apologize, make sure it is sincere and heartfelt. Doesn't the other person deserve to know that you messed up and you regret it? When you can manage a sincere apology, tensions can evaporate and people disarm like magic. Hopefully, knowing the power of a genuine and much-needed apology will make it a little easier for you to deliver one.

One of the biggest mistakes almost all of us make when we apologize is adding the word "but" after the apology. Sometimes our intentions are good and sometimes our inside voice is the culprit - but either way you should steer clear of "but."

Instead of this:

✗ I am sorry that I asked you if you were ever going to stop talking in front of everyone, but you were going on and on and on and people were losing interest. I really was just trying to be helpful.

Say this:

✔ I am sorry I asked you if you were ever going to stop talking in front of our team. I was rude and I can understand why you would be upset.

When you use the word "but," you negate your apology and therefore have not actually apologized at all. Skip the "but;" if you are sorry, you are sorry. There is no need to rationalize why you did what you claim to regret.

Here are some other non-apologies that do more harm than good and certainly do not serve to enhance the relationship:

✗ I'm sorry you feel that way.

✗ I'm sorry you took it that way.

✗ I'm sorry you're angry.

When you add the word "you" after your "I'm sorry," you discredit your apology because you are essentially communicating that you are not actually sorry for what you said or did, you only wish that the other person didn't take it so personally or get so upset - and that sends the message that you think the other person is overreacting, which can only lead to defensive reactions. Not good. Just put yourself in the other person's shoes and ask yourself what your inside voice would be saying if somebody apologized to you in this way. I have been on the receiving end of each of these kinds of non-apologies (as I'm sure you have, as well); all they do is make me more upset! Far better to shut the duck up than to utter a lame non-apology like one of these. Apologies really fall flat when they are:

- ✗ *Insincere*. If you only apologize to try to diffuse a situation or appease someone who has demanded an apology, you will not come across as genuine and you may actually cause more damage to the relationship.

- ✗ *Not backed up*. If there is no effort on your part to make things right or change things going forward, you end up having to apologize repeatedly for the same behavior, which makes your apologies hollow and meaningless.

- ✗ *Unspecific*. If you say, "I'm sorry," but don't (or, worse, can't) say why, other people will know right away that your apology is phony and may start to think less of you for attempting to fool them with a fake "I'm sorry."

Okay, so we know what doesn't work when it comes to apologizing. Let's talk about the nuts and bolts of what *does* work. A good apology has three components to it:

- ✓ Own up to what you have said or done. If you called someone "difficult," you might just want to say, "I am sorry I called you 'difficult.' It was unkind of me."

- ✓ Own up to how the other person is affected by what you have said or done *without excuses*, such as: "I can understand why that would bother you."

- ✓ Make a commitment, either to the other person or to yourself, for things to be different in the future. For the apology to be sincere you have to change your behavior going forward. If, five minutes after the apology, you repeat the behavior, then your apology is meaningless.

It's also essential that you only apologize if you truly mean it. If you don't mean it, don't apologize. Remember that the goal here is to foster better workplace relationships by showing appreciation and being genuine - and nothing is less appreciative or more disingenuous than an insincere apology.

"It is easier to eat crow while it's still warm."

- Dan Heist[36]

When you discover that you have made a mistake, the best thing to do is to make amends ASAP. I don't want to imply that a late apology is worse than no apology, because that certainly isn't true, but apologies do typically need to be timely in order to have the most impact. Just like with tough talks (and for many of us, apologies definitely qualify as tough talks), the closer you can respond to the act in question, the more effective that response will be.

Here are some examples of great apologies to get you started:

- ✓ I'm sorry I called you "delusional." That was a rude thing to say. It won't happen again.
- ✓ I apologize for my tone during our conversation. I realize that it made it difficult for you to communicate with me.

- ✔ I apologize for making the "princess" comment in the meeting. I can understand why you were upset. [Then you inwardly commit to keeping your snarky jabs to yourself.]

- ✔ I'm sorry I yelled at you for messing up the figures. Not only did I behave rudely, I was wrong. In the future I will try harder to control my temper.

- ✔ I'm sorry for saying you were wasting time and telling you to use your common sense. That was an inappropriate way to express my concerns.

Top Tools to Recall: Building Relationships

- ✔ Adopt the 5:1 rule - five positive interactions for every one negative interaction. Build up those relationship bank accounts!

- ✔ Show appreciation, be humble and apologize when you need to.

- ✔ Be genuine. Always, always, always be genuine.

- ✔ Never stop trying...even if they are defensive or suspicious of your intentions. Perseverance pays off!

Can you hear the cheers and fanfare? Great job! You have learned everything you need to know to totally transform your difficult conversations in the workplace. I hope you are very proud of yourself - you have just accomplished something that a lot of people avoid for their entire lives!

Now, all you have to do is put your newfound skills into practice out in the real world. Don't worry if you aren't perfect at it yet. We all mess up (I know I do, frequently!). The point is that you are trying - and practice makes perfect!

> "There is more hunger for love and appreciation in the world than there is for bread."
>
> - Mother Teresa

Remember that all of us strive to fulfill our basic human needs to be heard, to be appreciated and to be respected. When you have that wisdom tucked in your back pocket, you can take it confidently into the workplace and use it to create some seriously productive conversations. Prepare to amaze yourself with what you can accomplish simply by communicating, listening and responding without judgment. A whole new world of smoother relationships and pleasant working environments await!

Best of luck to you!

Your Elephant in the Office "Cheat Sheet"

✓ *Be prepared.* Cool down and focus on the facts, then craft your ABC message: accurate, brief and clear.

✓ *Be curious.* You can't change what you don't know and neither can others. Listen attentively and let go of being "right." Expect to learn something new.

✓ *Be direct.* People would rather hear the truth even if it hurts. No spinning.

✓ *Be neutral.* No blame or "hot," judgmental language. Avoid reacting to defensiveness. This isn't personal.

✓ *Be brief.* Don't overwhelm people with too much information. Stick to your goal.

✓ *Be proud.* Choose not to get "hooked" even when provoked. It pays to take the high road.

✓ *Be patient.* Gratification is seldom instant. Watch the fruits of your labor unfold before you.

✓ *Be proactive.* Don't wait for issues to crop up. Foster positive working relationships by apologizing when necessary and showing genuine appreciation.

Recommended Reading

Below is a list of my favorite books. These are fabulous reads that have all inspired and/or taught me in one way or the other. I recommend you read them all!

- Stone, Douglas. Patton, Bruce. Heen, Sheila. ***Difficult Conversations.*** New York: Penguin Books, 2010.
- Ury, William. ***The Power of a Positive No.*** New York: Bantam Dell, 2007.
- Fisher, Roger. Ury, William. Patton, Bruce. ***Getting to Yes.*** New York: Penguin Books, 1991.
- Fisher, Roger. Shapiro, Daniel. ***Beyond Reason.*** New York: Penguin Books, 2006.
- Scott, Susan. ***Fierce Conversations.*** New York: Berkley Books, 2002.
- Patterson, Kerry. et al. ***Crucial Conversations.*** New York: McGraw Hill, 2002.
- Issacs, William. ***Dialogue: The Art of Thinking Together.*** New York: Doubleday, 1999.
- Tarvis, Carol. Aronson, Elliot. ***Mistakes Were Made (But Not by Me)***. Orlando: Harcourt Inc., 2007.
- Strand Ellison, Sharon. ***Taking the War Out of Our Words.*** Oregon, Wyatt-MacKenzie Publishing Inc., 2009.
- Crane, Thomas G. ***The Heart of Coaching.*** San Diego, FTA Press, 2002.

Endnotes

Introduction

1. Check out the programs at Harvard Law School: www.pon.harvard.edu

2. Zig Ziglar was a well-known motivational speaker and author whom we've quoted a few times throughout this book! Check out his website at www.ziglar.com.

Chapter 1: We Really Do Need to Talk

3. Quote is derived from: Steakley, John. *Armor*. New York, Daw Books, 1984.

Chapter 2: Avoid at Your Peril

4. *Brazilian loses more than hearing*: BBC News, World Edition (August 20, 2003). http://news.bbc.co.uk/w/healthy/3169049.stn

5. Anthony J. D'Angelo is the author of *Rich Grad, Poor Grad*. You can find out more about his work at http://www.collegiate-empowerment.org

6. Richard Pascale is a business consultant, scholar and the best-selling author of *The Power of Positive Deviance: How Unlikely Innovators Solve the World's Toughest Problems.*

Chapter 3: Nail the Real Issue

7. Martina Navritalova is a famous tennis player and the author of several books. Check out her website at: www.martinanavritalova.com

8. Alda. Alan. *Things I Overheard While Talking to Myself.* New York. Random House, 2007 (Kindle version). Retrieved from Amazon.com (lines 250-253).

Chapter 4: Hammer Out Your Goal

9. See Kathy's awesome, oft-quoted words at http://running.about.com/od/runninghumor/tp/goalsettingquotes.01.htm

10. Fitzhugh Dodson (1923-1993) was a world-famous psychologist, lecturer and author. He wrote many books including *The Art of Being a Parent.*

Chapter 5: Resist the Temptation

11. Franklin P. Jones was a Philadelphia reporter best known for writing huge numbers of often-quoted humorous and insightful anecdotes and sayings throughout his career.

12. H. Jackson Brown Jr. is the bestselling author of *Life's Little Instruction Book, Volumes I,II,III.* Nashville: Thomas Nelson (Kindle Version). Retrieved from Amazon.com.

Chapter 6: Designing Your ABC Message

13. David Livingstone (1813-1873, of "Dr. Livingstone, I presume?" fame) was a Scottish missionary who became famous for his explorations in Africa.

14. I have seen this formula referred to in many books and used by many consultants. I do not know the original author or origin of this formula.

15. François Fénelon (1651-1715) was a French writer and Roman Catholic Archbishop.

Chapter 7: Delivering Your ABC Message

16. Norman Cousins (1915-1990) was an American political writer who was well known for his peace advocacy, for which he won several awards.

Chapter 8: It's a Talk, not a Lecture

17. listening. Merriam-Webster.com (2012). http://Merriam-Webster.com (accessed: October 26, 2012).

Chapter 9: Dealing With Defenses

18. Benjamin Disraeli (1804-1881) dedicated over half of his life to government; he served as British Prime Minister twice over and was also one of the most eminent novelists of his time.

19. defensiveness. Dictionary.com Collins English Dictionary-Complete & unabridged 10th Edition. HarperCollins Publishers. http://dictionary.reference.com/browse/defensiveness (accessed October 26, 2012).

20. Tamm, James W. Luyet, Ronald. *Radical Collaboration*. New York: Harper, 2004 p. 28.

Chapter 10: Managing Freak-Outs

21. Jone Johnson Lewis. "Rita Mae Brown Quotes" About Women's History. http://womenshistory.about.com/od/quotes/a/rita_mae_brown.htm (accessed Oct 26, 2012).

22. *Seinfeld*. "The Opposite." Episode #86. Originally aired: Mary 19, 1994. Check it out for a giggle!

23. Thich Nhat Hanh is a Buddhist monk, author, poet and peace activist. Check out his website: http://www.plumvillage.org/thich-nhat-hanh.html

Chapter 11: Tool to Stay Cool

24. "Tools to Stay Cool" is inspired by what I learned from William Ury in his fantastic book, *The Power of a Positive No*. New York: Bantam Dell, 2007.

25. Kingman Brewster, Jr. (1919-1988) was an American scholar, educator and diplomat who is best known for his controversial leadership during his term as President of Yale University in the 1960s and 1970s.

Chapter 12: Tell Me More

26. John Marshall (1755-1835) was the fourth Chief Justice of the Supreme Court of the United States. As the longest-ever serving Chief Justice, he played an important role in the development of the modern American legal system.

Chapter 13: Respond, Don't React

27. Tamm, James W. Luyet, Ronald. *Radical Collaboration*. New York: Harper, 2004 p. 28.

28. Crowley, Katherine. Elster, Kathi. *Working With You Is Killing Me.* New York: Warner Business Books, 2006. This is a great book and you may want to buy it for yourself - just be careful about giving it to your nemesis!

29. Dorothy Nevill (1826-1913) was a noted writer and conversationalist who penned several memoirs.

Chapter 14: The Ultimate Power Tool

30. Gottman, J.M. *What Predicts Divorce? The relationship between marital processes and marital outcomes.* Hillside, N.J. Lawrence Erlbaum, 1994. You can check out John Gottman in action at http://www.youtube.com/watch?v=Xw9SE315GtA.

31. Losada, M. & Heaphy E. (2004) The role of positivity and connectivity in the performance of business teams: A nonlinear dynamics model. *American Behavioral Scientist*, 47(6), 740-765.

32. Also check out: Crane, Thomas G. *The Heart of Coaching.* San Diego: FTA Press, 2002 p. 166. He talks about the importance of providing significantly more supportive and appreciative feedback than you do suggestions for change. His ratio is 80% positive, reinforcing feedback and 20% constructive ideas for change.

33. William James (1842-1910) was an American physician and philosopher who is considered to be the founding father of the science of psychology in the United States.

34. Frank Tyger (1929-2011) was a famous American editorial cartoonist and humorist for the *Trenton Times* in New Jersey.

35. William Safire (1929-2009) was a Pulitzer Prize-winning writer who was a political columnist for the *New York Times* as well as a presidential speechwriter.

36. Get more pearls of wisdom from Dan Heist at http://www.searchquotes.com/quotes/author/Dan_Heist/

Made in the USA
Charleston, SC
30 March 2016